The Americans in Norfolk during World War Two

Over Here

Steve Snelling

Eastern Daily Press

The Breedon Books
Publishing Company
Derby

First published in Great Britain by
The Breedon Books Publishing Company Limited
Breedon House, 44 Friar Gate, Derby, DE1 1DA.
1996

Dedication

To my parents, who still remember the days when Norfolk was a
'Little America'.

Picture Credits

Eastern Counties Newspaper Archive: 6, 99, 105, 106, 107, 135, 138, 149, 193; H.Burks: 9;
C.Graves 7, 19, 181; J.Smith: 7, 10, 13, 16, 28, 29, 92, 94, 95, 185; T.Dungar: 16, 33, 141;
M.Jeffrey: 17, 18, 24, 93, 111, 112, 114, 160, 183, 184, 185, 189, 204; S.Adams: 17, 18, 22, 23,
26, 32, 37, 43, 55, 57, 59, 63, 74, 88, 93, 95, 96, 125, 126, 137, 152, 173, 174, 176, 183, 188;
M.Bowman: 19, 25, 32, 34, 36, 48, 74, 75, 76, 79, 102, 127; 2nd Air Division Memorial Library,
Norwich: 20, 58, 67, 68, 69, 70, 188; A.North Collection: 20, 21, 117, 118, 122, 127, 135, 136,
195; J.Archer: 22, 26, 27, 38, 61, 75, 82, 101; P.Everson, 448th Bomber Group Collection: 24,
28, 31, 33, 37, 51, 53, 58, 59, 61, 62, 64, 72, 73, 81, 88, 90, 115, 116, 123, 125, 152, 154, 155,
165, 166, 203; K.Thomas: 25, 38, 190; Crouch: 30; P.Ramm: 30, 78, 79, 83, 100, 105; 100th
Bomber Group Memorial Museum, Thorpe Abbotts: 60, 81, 83, 84, 85, 86, 155; 96th Bomber
Group Museum, Eccles Hall, via G.Ward: 30, 31, 39, 40, 41, 62, 80, 94, 104, 112, 118, 120, 121,
122, 124, 137, 186, 191, 192, 194; E.Brighty: 45; E.Wasson: 46; M.Holmes: 46, 47; J.Miller: 47;
Wartime Watton Museum, via K.Godfrey: 50, 91, 136, 164; B.Fisher: 50; D.Duffield: 52, 53, 120,
140, 190; W.O'Neil: 52; C.Warren: 65; A.Hoar: 66, 82, 142, 144, 146, 147; D.Hastings: 89, 178,
201, 202, 203; 352nd Fighter Group Association: 109, 110; R.Collis: 116, 148, 149; F.Carr: 119;
J.Ives: 129; R.Neumunz: 130, 131; R.Lindsay: 132, 133; B.Watson: 151; W.Cole: 158, 163;
R.Gustafson: 159; via R.Lawson: 167, 168, 169, 170, 171; S.Vandenberg: 172, 175; Lord
Walpole: 184; H.Godges: 185; A.Crook: 189; A.Bingham: 195.

Thanks also to *Eastern Daily Press* photographers Dennis Whitehead, Simon Finlay, Bill Smith
and Simon Lunt, and to Diane Townsend, Jackie Burrows and Kerry Elden of the Eastern
Counties Newspaper Photographic Department for their expert help.

ISBN 1 85983 066 8

Printed and bound by Butler & Tanner Ltd., Selwood Printing
Works, Caxton Road, Frome, Somerset.

Colour separations by Colour Services, Wigston, Leicester.

Jackets printed by Lawrence-Allen, Weston-super-Mare, Avon.

Contents

Introduction

THE historic market town of Wymondham, slumbering peacefully on a Sunday afternoon in the fourth wearying year of the war, was about to be transformed out of all recognition. Not that anyone realised it at first. Least of all Pamela Standley.

But as she walked with her friends along Market Street, she could hardly fail to notice the stirrings of change that presented itself in the shape of two young servicemen in khaki uniform.

Nothing strange in that, except that these uniforms were nothing like the coarse, ungainly uniforms worn by British soldiers. They were smart and tailored. There was a sense of opulence about them which seemed almost out of place amid the drab austerity of rationed Norfolk. It was only the following day that the two girls realised that the men they had seen had been Yanks from the nearby United States Army Air Force base at Hethel.

Fields of cows give way to the fields of 'Little America'. Only a hedge separates farmer Ralph Fisher's dairy herd from Liberators of the 467th BG at Rackheath. Mr Fisher's family lived in a converted railway carriage on Green Lane within yards of the end of the runway, having been granted permission to remain there 'at their own risk'. The B-24 to the right of the tree is the *Belle of the East*.

To them, those two young Americans represented the vanguard of a 'Friendly Invasion' which would alter their lives, and the lives of thousands more people like them, and provide for many their most indelible memories of World War Two.

Pamela Standley recalls: "Nobody who hadn't seen it would believe how changed Wymondham became once Hethel was fully operational. About 7pm every evening, the town filled up with Yanks pouring in, some in trucks, but an awful lot on cycles, a mode of transport that did not seem very familiar to lots of them. The cinema was full every night, all the pubs were overflowing, the dances were packed."

Wymondham's transformation was, in microcosm, what was happening all over Norfolk. By early 1944, the county was criss-crossed by a network of air strips around which hutted encampments had grown into fully-fledged bases, many of them dwarfing the neighbouring rural communities from which they took their names. The fields of Norfolk became a 'Little America' as the 8th Air Force, the Mighty Eighth, joined with the RAF Bomber Command in carrying the war into the heart of Hitler's much-vaunted Reich.

The 2nd and 3rd Air Divisions, representing the spearhead of their country's greatest strategic bombing force, together with their fighter escorts, occupied no fewer than 17 bases throughout Norfolk: Attlebridge, Bodney, Deopham Green, East Wretham, Hardwick, Hethel, Horsham St Faith, North Pickenham, Old

Wheels down, a B-24 sweeps across a field and over a hedge to land at rural Hardwick.

American airmen from Hethel making friends in a local pub.

FROM
SOMEWHERE   IN ENGLAND

THE
67th

BOMBARDMENT
SQUADRON

THE
44th

BOMBARDMENT
GROUP
WISHES YOU

From Somewhere in England ...or to be precise, from Shipdham in Norfolk. A Christmas card designed on the base which was sent by an airman to a local family.

Buckenham, Rackheath, Seething, Shipdham, Snetterton, Thorpe Abbotts, Tibenham, Watton and Wendling.

Their contribution to the war effort was immense, and so was their sacrifice. No fewer than 6,300 men from the exclusively Norfolk-based 2nd Air Division lost their lives in the conflict. But no less telling than their combat endeavours was their impact on the social fabric of everyday life in Norfolk. Their sheer vitality and generosity of spirit produced an intoxicating atmosphere, and it is a measure of its bright, burning intensity that, more than half a century later, the special relationship still endures as one of the shining legacies of that most terrible of conflicts.

That it is a two-way feeling is evidenced in countless letters from former American airmen. Harold Burks, who served as a radio operator in the 93rd Bombardment Group, records: "Memories of events during the war tend to become kaleidoscopic. I remember how cold the

Nissen hut was, and how poor our mess food was, and the sense of dread at three o'clock in the morning when preparing for a mission. The seemingly endless wait to take off after being briefed. I remember the pubs as oases of cheer and good fellowship. Most of all, I remember the fundamental decency of the English people under very trying circumstances. Every return trip to Norwich has reconfirmed this memory, and my 'love affair' is rekindled."

This book is both a product and a reflection of that unique relationship. It is not a comprehensive history, neither is it a combat record. Such works already exist in great numbers, among the most prominent being those written by East Anglian historians Roger Freeman and Martin Bowman.

The emphasis here is, unashamedly, parochial. There is little here about grand strategy. Our focus is on the human element and the impact of transplanting thousands of Americans into the heart of Norfolk. Yet it is impossible to ignore the operational element, and we have sought to reflect this in a series of graphic personal accounts.

Drawing on the archives of the *Eastern Daily Press*, the 2nd Air Division Memorial Library in Norwich and a host of private sources, *Over Here* seeks to commemorate and pay tribute to Norfolk's proud wartime association with the men and women of the US 8th Air Force.

Every attempt has been made to provide a cross-section of life during this brief yet extraordinary period in our county's history. Some bases have undoubtedly fared better than others in this record. The events described and photographs reproduced, however, should be viewed merely as examples of what occurred throughout Norfolk.

More than any other book produced in this series, *Over Here* has been a team effort, and it is fair to say that without the help of a great many people, on both sides of the Atlantic, it would not have been possible. While it would take another volume to name everyone who has assisted, I must recognise the great help and

Home from home. Harold Burks, left, cutting the grass outside his Nissen hut at Hardwick. Such huts were typical of the rudimentary quarters most Americans found themselves in when they reached Norfolk.

support given by the following: Phyllis DuBois (2nd Air Division Memorial Trust librarian), David Hastings (2nd AD Memorial Trustee), Steve Adams, John Archer, Ron Batley, Martin Bowman, Bud Chamberlain (2nd AD Association), Bob Collis (Norfolk & Suffolk Aviation Museum), Dennis Duffield, Tommy Dungar, Pat Everson, Ken Godfrey, Evan Harris, Martin Jeffrey, Richard Lindsay, Pat Ramm, Jonathan Smith, Keith Thomas, Geoff Ward and Charles Warren.

Full acknowledgement must also be given to Willis S.Cole Jr, of Washington State, who generously provided the account of the only Medal of Honor mission flown from a Norfolk air base which is to form the basis of a book he is writing. I am also indebted to Anne Hoare for permission to make full use of her research on the the American Army Air Force Hospital at Wymondham College.

Finally, my thanks go to all those who contributed material for this book. Selecting which items to use has been the hardest task of all and I am only sorry there has not been room to include everything.

Steve Snelling,
Norwich,
August 1996.

Letters Home

Roy Jonasson, an air mechanic with 564th Squadron, 389th Bombardment Group, arrived at Hethel air base on July 7, 1943. At 37, 'Jon', as he was nicknamed, was a good deal older than the average GI. Throughout his 22-month stay at the Norfolk base, he maintained a regular correspondence with his wife, Mildred, who he had married in 1942.

His letters, now preserved in the 2nd Air Division Memorial Library, present a graphic portrait of life on a wartime bomber base. A man of high ideals, his reflections on the relationship between US airmen and their Norfolk neighbours are in stark contrast to the popular image of Americans in Britain being 'over-sexed, over-paid, and over here'...

Roy Jonasson, far left back row, and colleagues from Hethel with a group of local children.

July 16, 1943

...Night before last Bill Holland, Chauncey Strop, Pat and Jim and I went to town for the first time. Our pass was good from 6.30 pm to 11pm.

They allow 2 of us to go at a time in the evening and our means of transportation is by GI trucks. It took us about one half-hour to get to town.

On the way...we travel on very narrow roads, hardly room for two cars to pass...Most transportation is by bicycle or foot. The bicycle is very common in town and in the country. They also use double-decker buses in the towns we visited.

We passed many small farms. The houses have long straw roofs like you have seen in the pictures, lots of green meadows with high stone or brick walls especially along the roadsides. Usually vines are creeping over the walls...

Upon arriving in town we stopped at a Tavern and had supper. The place reminded me so much of the English place you and I ate supper one evening in Denver...Everything was the same, except here the food was scarce. We had boiled potatoes (they call them 'pots'), veal steak ground up into patties (about 15% meat and 85% bread and crackers), English tea (very good), raspberry tarts for dessert, dark bread (no butter), and oxtail soup. We surely did enjoy the meal.

August 15, 1943

...Night before last one of the fellows went out into the meadow and picked a cup full of blackberries which we ate the following morning on our puffed wheat. It took us a little longer to pick them as we ate a lot while picking them.

These berries are just getting ripe now and there is going to be a lot of them. This used to be an old English estate at one time and certain sections of it are still very beautiful. Last evening Bill Chauncey, Jim and myself took a ride on our bikes through the estate and the country roads and I have never before seen so many beautiful English roads. They are very narrow...but we saw many small English country homes with little old white fences around them, long green hedges lining the boundaries of the wheat fields, the pastures, the vegetable gardens, etc. We went down one beautiful narrow road...There were trees on both sides and down at the turn of the road was an old English home with the little white wooden fence in front of the house. It was so picturesque. As I pedalled along I could not help but think of you and how happy I will be when I can get back to you. How I would have loved to have had you along...One can easily see that the standard of living here is much lower than in the States but the people seem to be happier.

The bombers are certainly roaring and flying tonight and it is quite a sight. We sure like to hear and see them fly as it means that the war will end that much sooner...I really feel fine as usual except for the homesickness and missing you all the time but I feel better because the war seems to be speeding up to a fast finish...

September 17, 1943

...Wednesday, Sgt Lyons and Sgt Switzer and I went to Norwich. We arrived about noon time and had a good dinner in comparison to what we get here.

We then went to the show and saw *Hello Frisco, Hello!* a musical and I sure enjoyed it. Then we went shopping and believe me, dear, there is not much to buy in these stores. You have to have coupons for most things, which we do not have. I did find and bought two dozen nice English Christmas cards and am sending them on to you...Well, dear, it seems funny but the blackberries are still ripening and getting thicker than ever and the leaves are still on the trees, though it is cooler here. While in town we priced the grapes and they were 12 shillings a pound ($2.40), the same grapes we find for five cents a pound in California.

September 19, 1943

...I pedalled to a little town six miles away by the name of Hethersett, a beautiful little English village. It was about 5.50pm at that time and as I approached...coming down the narrow, winding road I could hear the church chimes in the distance. As I got nearer, the chimes were clearer and when I got around the bend in the road I could see the little English church sitting on the side of the hill. It was one of the most beautiful sights I have ever seen. The church on the hill, and lower down the sheep were grazing in the green meadow. There was a cemetery just outside the church, at one side, and we saw the most beautiful sunset... I decided to go into the church. I found it somewhat similar to our church...The most interesting thing I noticed was that the people were there for a reason, to give thanks. They let me know that I was welcome but that was all. They do not gather after church. They all walked out solemnly. You could tell that they have had the test and have come through with flying colors. I liked it so well that I shall go there again when I have the chance.

It is much cooler now and we can see the approach of Fall and Winter. We are wearing our heavy underwear. I just looked out the door and some planes went over. It is very dark but the sky is very clear and the stars are all twinkling. The Axis will get some more bombs tonight...

November 15, 1943

...the Germans are fighting hard now because they have to. But they seem to be standing on their last legs.

Sgt James Adovacio and Sgt Billy Apel were both killed in a flight and both were mechanics at Biggs Field, El Paso... Lieut E.L.Fowble, the officer in whose plane I rode to Denver, was killed. He sure was a swell officer and pilot. Also killed was Lieut Bisetti, the pilot of the plane in which I took a ride here in England.

Night before last we had our first sign of snow but it melted as soon as it fell. The last two days have been real cold, rainy, damp and windy. It has blown most of the time. One feels the cold here much more than in Montana where it gets much colder, but in Montana it is a dry cold.

The long johns finally won out about a week ago. Now I am wearing them all of the time and the rest of the boys are doing the same...

December 1, 1943

I have just returned from Norwich as this was my day off... I saw two good motion pictures. Afterwards, I went up to the restaurant where I always eat and had a good supper. Gee, how I would have loved to have had you along.

The place where I eat is a pretty little homey tavern and it is always busy. They have little lamps about the tables. For dinner I had a pot of tea, two sausages and mash. 'Mash' in English means mashed potatoes. And I had bread and jam. After eating I caught the 5.15pm bus and got off... at Bowling Green, a small country village where we take a side road that leads to the base. It was dark, but full moonlight. I could hear the English children singing songs about Jesus as I walked up the winding, narrow, muddy English lane. It was very beautiful and got me thinking. Here we are, our work is to kill people and what a blessed thing it would be to have peace on earth again.

The more I become acquainted with the English people and the more I observe them, I find them to be polite, clean and hard working... They appear to be peace-loving people and one never hears them complain...

December 26, 1943

We had our Christmas dinner anywhere from 11am to 2pm. Bill and I ate last, about 1.30pm and I must say it was one of the best dinners I have had in the Army. We had turkey, potatoes, peas, cranberries (sauce), gravy, very good rice soup (with chicken broth), and yellow cake with chocolate icing (the first cake we ever had over here from GI). When we finished eating we could hardly walk back to the line. Why, I just waddled back! In the afternoon our Base had about 300 English orphans as guests to a Christmas party in the Mess Hall. We have been saving candy, etc,

for a long time for this event and I can say that we sure made a lot of children happy. They were brought in by our Army trucks which picked them up from the nearby villages.

Last night, Bill, Jim, Jack and I had an invitation to an English home for dinner. We left here at 6pm on our bicycles and arrived in Hethersett at about 6.30pm. There was lots of mud all the way as we rode along. The dinner was at the home of two old ladies, one about 55 and the other about 60. Her son was in the RAF and was home on furlough and we had a most enjoyable evening...

So many things flashed in my mind as I sat down in the old English chair and the more I looked around the more I thought of long ago and the more I saw. The furniture was rather crude but so homey and nice. There were the English pictures, the fireplace with the tea kettle steaming away over the fire supported by an iron stand, the dishes hanging here and there on the walls, and so many other things — plain but beautiful.

One of the ladies wore a black skirt with a purple sweater (both looked worn a lot) and the other wore a slip-over blue apron with sleeves. As I sat there eating I thought of the many things they had gone through during the Blitz, yet they were so happy to have some Yanks in their home for Christmas. The home was entirely a poor woman's home but everything was so nice and clean and one could not have fixed a better home with a lot of money. Much of their silverware, furniture, pictures, chairs, tables, sewing machine, etc, were very old.

After getting warm in the living room by the fire she called us to the kitchen to eat. It sounded so funny when she said, 'Come along, Jon! Bill! Jim! and Jack!'... She asked us if we liked everything on one plate and we said yes. The Norfolk way is to eat your Yorkshire pudding and gravy first and then, when you finish that, you eat your vegetable and meat and so on down the line... After we finished eating what was on our plates they brought out a big tall English plum pudding and was it good! They tell us they get only ½lb of raisins per month. After eating the

Mildred Jonasson in military pose.

plum pudding they served tea. Hurrah! With the tea, we had mince pie!

After dinner we went into the living room and they brought out the *Coronation Book of the King and Queen of England* when they were crowned in 1936 or 1937. It was so interesting... I must say I shall never forget the happy Christmas these two old ladies gave me...

March 5, 1944
...The last few days we have had the heaviest snow fall so far this year and it has remained on the ground the longest period of time. The planes really looked pretty in the snow. Of course, it makes that much more work for the ground crew... The woods look so pretty with all the snow on the fir trees and bushes. You could see the cotton-tail rabbits hopping about in the snow looking for something to eat. There are also lots of pheasants around this section of England and lots of small game and good hunting. Hunting is not permitted in any form and that is probably the reason there are so many various kinds of game birds here...

Tonight it is real clear and the stars are shining so brightly and it is nearly full moon. There is not a sound of a plane or the sight of a searchlight beam. All seems so peaceful. None would ever dream that there is a war on...

March 28, 1944
...Outside it is real foggy but I can hear many planes in the air getting their formations for another day's work of routine bombing.

At our shelter door I heard a sharp meow and one of our base cats wanted in so now he is peacefully asleep on one of the boy's cots after a night of extensive manoeuvring. I wonder if he found much flak in his mission. He was just a kitten when he first came here and now he is full grown. He is a pretty cat. This is just one of many. We have several dogs on the Base also raised from puppies. Some were brought over from the States, some bought here. We like all of them and how they like to go with the fellows! They know when it is chow time, too. How they like to ride in our vehicles...

April 2, 1944
...The other morning I was out early in the dispersal area and we were getting our planes preflighted for an early mission. I had to pick up two batteries for one of the planes as the battery had run down. When I was unloading them into the bomb bay section one of the officers asked me if we had just received this plane. I told him it had been here a couple of days. Well, I went on up to the flight deck. Afterwards I found out it was Jimmy Stewart. He is a major. He made the flight to Berlin...

April 12, 1944
...Our food at times has been very poor and slices of plain bread alone tasted good to us. The censor will probably cut this out. There are many things I'll be able to tell you when I get home. Again, some days we get lots of good food. But we have nothing to kick about as there are others much worse off. When we go to town we always get filled up with fish and chips and then eat at the Red Cross, and then go out somewhere else and eat more...

May 2, 1944

...Last Saturday was my day off and I remained around the barrack until around 3pm. Then I decided to go to (censored) on my bicycle. I saw a parade and exercises in a park called the Kings' Meadow.

A number of men from our four squadrons took part in the parade and were reviewed by Lord Ironside, a British Field Marshal from the last World War... This was my first visit to this village and I enjoyed it very much with its old historical buildings, Abbey, etc. An elderly Englishman by the name of Whiting showed me about the town and invited me to tea in his home which I did not accept as I wished to see the parade...

May 9, 1944

...This afternoon General Doolittle and General Spaatz were here at our base and put on a little program of speeches and presented our Group with the Citation (organisation) from the President, etc. These officers were three-starred generals. While on the base they took motion pictures for the newsreel out in our dispersal area, and at various other places on our base.

At the speaker's stand, to one side, was *Old Blister Butt*, *Old Irish*, and *Miss Liberty*, planes of our squadron which have seen lots of action. Watch for the newsreel. These planes have lots of history behind them...

July 24, 1944

...It is now 9.20pm and I just came in this moment from the dispersal area. As I pedalled up the winding road I was whistling and looking about noticing the horses and cows grazing peacefully in the green pastures. The first thought that came to my mind was how thankful I was that you were over there where it was peaceful and safe. And how nice it will be to be back once again to that peace. I thought of the Saturday nights I had put in the store and here nearly every night is a Saturday night, or much longer of late. But we like it that way because the Nazis are getting the punches where it hurts and

at the right time and when it does the most harm...

September 18, 1944

Yesterday, all day and most of last night up to 1 o'clock this morning was very, very busy. Today's news told the reason (*airborne assault on Arnhem*)... We had plenty of extra work given to us and we finished it in good time as planned. Every man did his work like a veteran, although most of us were very tired.

The base would remind you of a main street downtown on a Saturday night, only all work. All kinds of lights were burning and the colored lights on the fuel trucks and trailers, and the various colored lights on our planes as they come in and taxi about, and the lights on the vehicles.

Yesterday I met a sergeant from our Squadron who went down over Ploesti about a year ago last August. He was on Lieut Hughes' crew. Lieut Hughes' wife received, posthumously, his Congressional Medal of Honor. The sergeant was the only one to get out. He had several burned areas (scars) about his hands, face and body. But he seemed to be so cheerful and happy. He had been held prisoner for some time and was freed when the Russians broke into Rumania...

How I would love to be with you tonight at Denver, even if it is frosty there... The war still continues to go our way rapidly and should come to a climax here soon. I do not believe we will leave over here before Christmas... But I am not disappointed as we could get into some very bad places in the Far East...

September 24, 1944

...I believe we are passing through our most critical period over here for the Germans are desperate, yet still have strength and with their fanatical leaders they will try anything and anything goes in this war! I have seen what their buzz bombs and rockets will do to the innocent civilian families and their homes and belongings that it has taken a life time to accumulate. Anyway, soon they will be at their end, so far as a warring nation is concerned.

Yesterday was our Open House day and our 200th mission celebration and some of the planes flew in formations. And then we sent some of them out on combat missions... We really had a nice meal for supper... It was really better cooked and prepared than the dinner at Christmas or Thanksgiving. We had chicken, potatoes, cut-up celery, and lettuce and tomatoes, ice cream, cake and coffee and bread and butter. In the afternoon they had a program in which Generals Doolittle, Spaatz, Timberlake took part. Also, a number of high-ranking British officers took part, and an Egyptian and a Chinese officer. We also had a squadron of P-51 fighter planes put on flying stunts...

October 5, 1944
I have been spending the first part of my furlough here at Yarmouth, a coastal town along the North Sea. I really like it here as there is a very good ocean breeze which seems to make one feel so good.

Yarmouth reminds me of Balboa Beach a lot, except there are no concessions and it is not commercialised. Many of the homes and buildings have been destroyed but the people go on as usual about their business and chores... Here at Yarmouth I spend most of my time eating, sleeping and going down to the pier to watch the boats come and go and the fishermen. I am having such a grand time.

Dearest, so many times I think of you and wish you were here along with me. Then I think that one of these days you will be with me and what a grand day that will be. You see, dearest, you are my 'Lilli Marlene'...

December 23, 1944
...I sit here at the supply in the dispersal area and am listening to the planes as they pass overhead tonight and it makes you wonder, at this time of year. Christmas! A time that should bring joy, goodwill and peace to all men and instead all of us are doing our best to do away with man and material of our enemy. It does make one wonder.

Yesterday we had a great number of English children at our base from the surrounding villages for a Christmas party. And what lovely children they were, so polite, clean, poor but so cheerful, and in old clothing, though it was clean and neat. I can say that we men had as much fun as the children... I nearly adopted one to bring back to you! And I love them just as much... Many were orphan children. We had a Santa Claus for them and candy...

Everywhere one goes he finds the American soldier putting on a Christmas party for the children... Yes, we continue stronger than ever with our work and operations but this is a little of the real Christmas spirit given to our Allies, especially to those who have nothing, or who have lost much. What a great day it will be for all when we get peace once and for all and we can come back to the ones we love and miss so much...

March 20, 1945
...It has been another beautiful day from early morning. As the sun came up I saw more V2s from the East leaving their corkscrew vapor trails, all silvery and beautiful in the early light. Now the sun is setting again. Our horseshoe games give us a little something different to do and make us feel so much better. I am not very good at this game but we all have lots of fun, whether we win or lose...

This world is certainly made up of so many beautiful sights. There is so much to see about and I am so thankful we have the eyes to see so many beautiful things, beautiful in many different ways. By that I do not only mean the appearance of beauty in its outward form but the beauty also of that which is within one. And I am so happy to be able to see all of this beauty with you the rest of our life!

... In reasonable time our wishes will come true and I'll be back with you forever.

Give my love to the folks and be of good cheer. I know it is hard for you but soon, soon, our day will come.

Base Life

A lone bugler heralded the beginning of a new era in Anglo-American relations at Hethel air base on August 23, 1943. The Stars and Stripes are raised over Station 114 to mark its official transfer from the RAF, a detachment of which are parading in the background.

Sir Edward and Lady Stracey brought their young daughter in their Rover, complete with black-out headlight, to watch the 'flag ceremony' on April 12, 1944 at the base which mushroomed on Sir Edward's Rackheath estate. In all some nine tenant farms were swallowed up by the airfield complex which became home to the 467th BG.

A unit of the 452nd BG march through a wintry Norfolk countryside, led by their squadron colours, for a parade at Deopham Green.

Mud, glorious mud. When it rained — and it appeared to the American airmen arriving in Norfolk to do so with alarming regularity — many of the bases soon dissolved into quagmires. Here, one of the Irish navvies who helped build Shipdham airfield on farmland owned by the Patterson family struggles through a sea of mud. The date is January 27, 1943, the same day B-24s from the 44th BG launched their first attack on Germany from the base.

A line of boots on 'Mudville Heights' at Shipdham tell their own story. The men tried to keep their huts clean by leaving their boots outside.

Sgt Ferris Parsons, serving with the 452nd BG at Deopham Green, provided his own commentary on the conditions. Years after the war, Benjamin L.Everett, who had been based at Seething, recalled: "Some wise guy made the remark that this place is 'Seething in mud'. How right he was ...The floor of the mess hall was always about a half-inch deep in soupy mud. They would hose down the floor after each meal, but the water would not dry before the next meal so it was a never ending thing."

Early Daze at Deopham Green
By Sgt. Ferris Parsons

Unsung heroes. A ground crew loading bombs on to a 93rd BG Liberator at Hardwick. Crew chief T/Sgt Charles I.Graves recalls how his men would have to get out of bed at 2am on cold nights to 'pre-flight our aircraft prior to a mission to be sure everything was OK'.

Eyes, shielded from the sun, search the skies for the first sign of returning B-24s at Shipdham on May 14, 1943. It would be a long and agonising wait. On that day, 19 Liberators of the 44th BG had rendezvoused off Cromer with a force of B-17s to attack the heavily-defended port of Kiel. Almost a third, six aircraft, did not return. Major Howard 'Pappy' Moore, seen here in the foreground wearing sunglasses, had been on leave and although he arrived back at Shipdham in time for the briefing, he was too late to go on the mission, a fact which may well have saved his life. After Kiel, his aircraft, the famous *Suzy Q,* was the only survivor of the original 67th Squadron which had made the flight across the Atlantic the previous October.

Wheels down, the *Angel,* a 467th BG B-24, casts its shadow on Rackheath runway as it returns from a sortie.

Officers and men of the 389th BG swarm on and around a B-24 at Hethel prior to forming up for a formal photograph to mark the presentation of a Distinguished Unit Citation on May 9, 1944 (see Roy Jonasson's letters).

As a well-established former RAF base, Horsham St Faith had some of the best facilities for aircraft and men. This giant hangar, which still survives on what is now Norwich airport, is here housing *The Pied Piper* from the 458th BG.

The camouflaged, brick-built officers' mess at Horsham was the envy of many USAAF bases carved out of the Norfolk countryside. Many years after the war, the building was converted to house students from the University of East Anglia.

Lining the control tower at Hardwick. Note the signal flare which has just been shot off.

Images of family life adorn this underground air-raid shelter at Shipdham complete with fireplace and mantlepiece. As well as such home comforts as armchairs, they also had built-in bunks where ground crews slept rather than face the trek back to their huts.

A good illustration of the cramped men's quarters with central stove pipe. This one at Shipdham housed the 67th Bomb Squadron armaments section but was typical of hundreds of other Nissen-hutted barracks.

Pretty as a postcard, but the winter snows spelled only more hardships for the men of the USAAF in Norfolk. One of the two aircraft seen here at a Shipdham dispersal point during the harsh winter of 1944-45 is the B-24 *Gipsy Queen*. The hut, built to give ground crews some shelter, was constructed out of old bomb crates. One airman recalled how they were issued with only one bucket of coke each day to warm their quarters. Writing home from Seething in November, 1944, crew chief Harry Holmberg stated: "It's really cold here now, and we had our first snow the other day. The damn wind just keeps blowing all the time. I sure dread staying here another winter and freezing. It's so damp it just creeps into your bones."

On parade, outside the headquarters of the 452nd BG at Deopham Green.

Stylish wall art was to become a feature of the USAAF bases in Britain. This dramatic example decorated the fireplace wall of the Officers' Club at Seething from early 1944. 'The Griffon — Chaos from Aloft' was originally intended as the 448th BG's official insignia, but was never adopted. The white bar showed the Group's tally of bombing missions and enemy aircraft claimed as shot down. The club walls also carried a ten-picture mural depicting the story of a typical mission. It took almost three months to complete, and one of the artists later recalled: "We painted mostly at night, between 10 and 12 midnight, when the club was mostly deserted and very cold. The walls were even colder! At one time, Col Thompson dismissed us from our regular duties, in order to concentrate full-time on the murals..."

When it came to communication, some of the USAAF bases were way ahead of their time. This eye-catching information display panel was at North Pickenham.

Piping hot mugs of coffee, a tray of doughnuts and a pretty girl with charming smile to serve them up. No wonder these GIs at Old Buckenham were smiling. The pots of flowers on the hatches of the *Rhode Island* Red Cross Clubmobile were an usual feature, and that hand-held sign bidding GIs to 'Please take dirty cups to MP at side door' was surely a joke.

Queuing with a difference at Hardwick, with Pappy Dupasquale, Dave Wright and Mel Morrison playing up to the camera.

War or no war, there was always time for building snowmen when winter closed in. Everett Lord and Jack Hunter were responsible for the two roly-poly models at Shipdham.

A running snowball fight at Thorpe Abbotts offers an opportunity to release pent-up energy — and stay warm!

Each base had its own menagerie of cats and dogs, but Snetterton and Thorpe Abbotts went one better with their own donkeys. They were brought back to Norfolk from North Africa in August 1943, following the two Groups' involvement in the so-called 'Regensburg Shuttle' mission. The picture shows Lady Moe, who briefly became the mascot of the 100th BG. She was smuggled into Thorpe Abbotts aboard Lieut Owen 'Cowboy' Roane's B-17 and had to be administered with oxygen during the flight over the Alps. Despite Roane being reprimanded by the Ministry of Agriculture for breaching quarantine rules, 'Moe' remained on the base until her death the following winter when she succumbed either to the cold or, as some believed, to eating too much gum!

This well-trained duo, Dinghy and Smokey by name, belonged to ground crews at Hethel. Note the makeshift shack to the left. These were put up along the flight lines to give ground crews a modicum of shelter from the elements.

A Mass for the dead held in the chapel at Seething. The film star Jimmy Stewart, who was based at Tibenham and Old Buckenham, was one of many airmen who turned to religion as the deadly realities of war struck home.

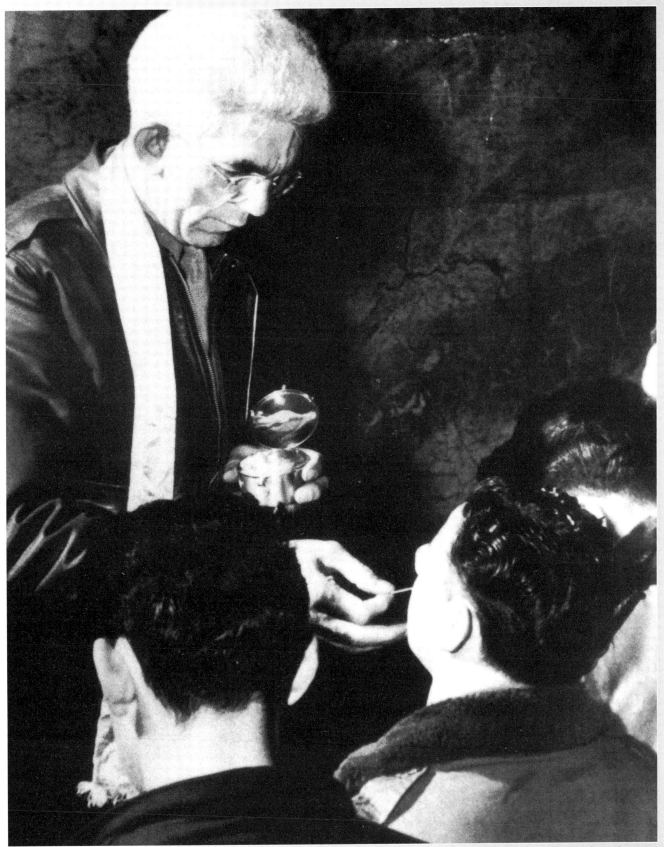

The Roman Catholic chaplain, seen here, giving Holy Communion to airmen of the 389th BG at Hethel before they set out on a combat mission, became a legendary figure in the 8th Air Force. Father Gerald Beck, known to his flock as 'White Flak', joined the Group in North Africa. His jeep was called *Hellzapoppin* and he referred to God as the 'First Pilot'. He flew a number of missions, earning the Air Medal, in order, he claimed, to better understand what the men had to endure. On one notable occasion, he even gave Holy Communion in the air during a bombing mission. Eventually, the head chaplain in Europe put a stop to his flying career.

Father Beck's chapel at Hethel was adorned by this mural of the Crucifixion which still survives to this day. It was painted in early 1944 by Beck's assistant, Charles W. 'Bud' Doyle, who later recalled: "I couldn't find a proper picture to use as a model ...so finally used the Crucifix on the end of my Rosary. When I finished I asked Father Beck if it was all right, and he informed me I neglected crossing the feet, but not to worry nobody would notice, which was wishful thinking because there were running comments on the subject."

Gone fishing! Two ground crew members of the 96th BG, based at Snetterton, pose with their impressive catch, a pike landed from Quidenham Lake.

Thousands of dollars exchanged hands every week in bases all over Norfolk as airmen tried out their luck in the nightly card games. This bunch of gamblers are members of the 453rd BG at Old Buckenham and include S/Sgt Bob Lucas, far right, with Charlie Wise next to him.

Distinctly less serious were such party games as 'apple-bobbing', seen here being performed by men of the 96th BG at Snetterton.

Large crowds could be guaranteed for the inter-base football matches. This one was between teams from Seething and Old Buckenham.

Baseball, inevitably, was another popular sport. This particular game staged at Shipdham on August 11, 1944 to mark the 44th BG's 200th mission, matched the Brass (officers higher than captains) against the The One Bars (those officers below captain's rank). One of the more unusual rules adopted for the day's festivities was that no badges of rank were to be worn. Anyone caught defying the order was to be put on KP (kitchen patrol), spud bashing and sweeping up!

Keep fit exercises of a different kind were the order of the day at Rackheath, as this photograph taken on July 26, 1944 reveals. The display of callisthenics in a field close to dispersal points was all part of Col Albert J.Shower's 'shaping-up programme.'

The English pub game of darts found its way on to the bases. Here a party of the 448th BG at Seething are chancing their arm. Bert La Point III, on extreme left, recalls: "We played a lot of darts on the base and in the pubs. Every time I played an Englishman ...for a beer (but) I only remember them having to buy me a beer once or twice during the 22 months I was based at Seething. From that, you can tell I wasn't a very good darts player." George Green, the man throwing the dart here, was killed in a road accident while serving at Seething.

An embarrassing moment for one GI, but a photograph which exemplifies the rural nature of many of the USAAF airfields in Norfolk. This evocative portrait was taken on Hall Farm, bordering the Rackheath base. Tractor driver Leslie Dungar and a Land Army girl can scarcely conceal their amusement as an airmen is caught short. The base guardroom can be seen on the left, with the hospital site in the background.

Cyclomania

Bicycles were big business on the USAAF bases around Norfolk during the war. As the war progressed and the number of cycles available diminished, prices soared. So highly prized was a personal bike that 'borrowing' became rife. Here at a vast 'bike park' established at Rackheath in October 1944, MPs are seen checking cycle numbers before returning many to their

rightful owners. Thomas S.Tinney, who flew with the 448th BG from Seething, recalls: "Bikes were a hot item as there weren't enough to go around and they weren't Government issued. It was quite a chore getting one. We would keep up with crews that were near their assigned number of missions and start bartering."

Ready, steady, go. The good, old-fashioned bicycle came into its own during the war. With fuel rationed and trucks in short supply, cycles became the chief mode of transport on and off the bases. Here, a 93rd BG combat crew led off by waist gunner S/Sgt T.J.Kilmer rides off for a briefing at Hardwick in April 1943.

Bikes litter the ground as members of the 458th BG gather around the Red Cross Clubmobile *Montana*, near Fifer's Lane on the edge of the Horsham St Faith base.

Above, left: A familiar sight in wartime Norfolk. Two Americans from the nearby Shipdham air base pedal up a banked country lane towards Southburgh Church.

Above, right: Each base had its own repair squads. This one is working at Seething.

Riding out from Seething, two members of the 448th BG pose outside the Cherry Tree pub. It was the kind of thatched building many Americans had expected to find as the norm when they headed out across the Atlantic.

A bicycle made for five is shown off by members of the 1916th Ordnance Ammunition Company based at Earsham. This unit was responsible for maintaining the bomb dumps dotted around the Norfolk-Suffolk border and for supplying bases as far afield as Shipdham and Parham.

A frosted up bicycle park in the 853rd Bomb Squadron area at North Pickenham in the winter of 1944-45.

Memorable Flights

OCTOBER 14, 1943 was destined to enter the annals of the USAAF as Black Thursday. On that day, a force of more than 250 bombers from the three bombardment Groups was dispatched against the ball-bearing plants at Schweinfurt.

The air battle which ensued in the skies over Germany was one of the bloodiest of the campaign. The target was effectively bombed but the cost was heavy. By the close of the day, a total of 60 B-17s were missing, another five battle-damaged bombers came down in England, 12 more struggled home to crash landings and 121 were in need of repair.

Among many stories of heroic deeds and devotion to duty, the courage of one Snetterton-based navigator stood out. Lieut Miles McFann flew aboard *Paper Doll* as a member of a 96th BG replacement crew led by Lieut Robert Bolick. And his actions during the USAAF's Mission 115 were to elevate him briefly to the status of national hero.

A few days after the raid, McFann gave his account of the epic flight in an interview broadcast to the United States. It was conducted by broadcaster Larry LeSueur and reflected the bombastic spirit of the times. The transcript is reproduced here:

LeSUEUR: "There's a new story going around London this week. It seems a German broadcaster was boasting about shooting down 60 of our planes the other day. But...at the end of the communique...he added sadly, 'One of our cities is missing.' Lieut Myles McFann, a 6ft 2½in oil

The crew of *Paper Doll* during training in the United States in May 1943. Miles McFann is far left, with Bob Downs, second left, and Robert Bolick, third right.

After completing his tour, Miles McFann joined the intelligence staff at Snetterton. He is seen here, far right, with Major Theo Dilz's crew on May 12, 1944, after they had just returned from the Zwickau oil refinery raid. The 96th BG lost 12 out of 26 aircraft dispatched, their highest loss in a single raid, and the strain of the mission is evident in the faces of the crew.

man from Eldorado, Arkansas, was navigator on one of the Fortresses that smashed Schweinfurt. He brought his plane back to England after the pilot was killed and the co-pilot wounded. Prime Minister Churchill was one of the first to hear McFann's story and now McFann will talk across the Atlantic to you. How did the Schweinfurt raid start off, Mac?"

McFANN: "Well, we headed across the English Channel with an escort of Thunderbolts. I was a little surprised that the Germans didn't put up much opposition at first, but as soon as the Thunderbolts left, the Germans caught up with us. Hermann Goering's squadron, the Happy Dolly Boys, piled in on us. The Germans seemed to have all their fighters concentrated on the approaches to Schweinfurt. Their guns were putting up a curtain of flak over the city so thick and

black we could have rolled our wheels on it. The Germans were desperate but they couldn't stop us."

LeSUEUR: "You think you got to Schweinfurt, eh?"

McFANN: "When we left Schweinfurt the factory was about 6,000 feet in the air."

LeSUEUR: "When did your troubles begin?"

McFANN: "Not until the formation was nearing the French coast on the way home. I was jumping up and down, taking a crack at the Germans and plotting our position on the map when we were hit by flak, rockets and cannon fire all at the same time. It just blew holes through the ship and pieces of shell cut off my oxygen mask. We fell out of formation. I tried to report the damage to the pilot. When I didn't get my answer I crawled into the cockpit. When I

Capt Miles McFann examining target photographs at Snetterton.

slipped in blood I knew what had happened. Our pilot was slumped over the controls and the co-pilot was trying to handle the ship with one hand. His other arm was broken and dangling. I tried to stop the pilot's bleeding with my hands, but couldn't. We carried him into the nose and Bombardier Edelstein put a tourniquet on his leg. I sat down at the controls next to the co-pilot. He held on to consciousness but was weakening fast. I knew I could handle the ship in the air, but I had never landed a Fortress."

LeSUEUR: "Why didn't you fellows bail out?"

McFANN: "Well, the pilot was dying and the co-pilot too badly hurt to be able to open a parachute. So we couldn't leave them."

LeSUEUR: "How'd you manage to get her down?"

McFANN: "Well, the co-pilot wouldn't let himself pass out. When I'd ask him what to do, he'd tell me. Two Spitfires picked us up and led us through the clouds. I came out 600 feet over the airfield. The co-pilot was too weak to push the controls but he guided my hands. After a while, he was too weak to talk. He'd just nod or shake his head. I made one run around the field

and he managed to say, "All right, set her down." I did and we only bounced once."

LeSUEUR: "Lieut McFann, everybody in the 8th Air Force, from General Eaker down, thinks you did a great job."

McFANN: "Well, I'd like to say a word for our rear gunner. During the whole battle and the landing, we couldn't get any word to him. He didn't know whether we were going to crash or bail out. He just stuck to his guns without asking any questions."

LeSUEUR: "I return you now to *Report to the Nation* in New York..."

McFann had landed *Paper Doll* at Ford, an RAF station near to the Sussex coast. The next day Winston Churchill, who was visiting the base to watch manoeuvres, was told of McFann's exploit and asked to be introduced to him. Despite the severity of his wounds, the co-pilot, Lieut Bob Downs, survived. McFann went on to complete his 25-mission tour. For his bravery and exceptional skill in bringing the B-17 safely home from Schweinfurt he was awarded the Silver Star.

Making Friends

JOHN W.McLane Jr served as a navigator with the 44th Bomb Group based at Shipdham. Between April and October 1944 he flew 31 combat missions before returning safely to the United States. During his tour of duty, he, like many young Americans far from home, formed a close attachment with a local family, and in particular a girl called Margaret, from west Norwich. Years later he recorded his memories of a friendship which helped sustain him through those difficult months. What follows is abridged from his account:

"After we had dated a time or two, Margaret asked me to cycle with her to meet her family. The house was one of a number of homes facing a large semi-circle cul-de-sac. Like everything British of that time frame, the yards were fastidiously neat. The father's name was William. His wife was a Cockney and still, after many years, had a distinct Cockney dialect. A lovelier couple has never been born. They welcomed me into their home as if I were their own son. There is no way I can explain what this meant to me during my tour of combat. To have a place where I was as welcome as if I were in my own home was a benefit to which no value can be assigned.

"It did not take too long to realise that the whole family was very disciplined as to what questions were asked of me. Never — I mean not once — did they ever ask me what I did, how I did it, what missions I had flown, where our next target would be, what were our tactics, or anything concerning our air base or planes, etc. I had the best of all lives if one has to be in combat. An orderly cleaned my room, made my bed and after a hard day's work, I could go to town, cycle to Margaret's family, have peace and quiet with no questions asked. The love and kindness was at times like an oasis in hell. I will love this family and the English people as long as I shall live.

"There was nothing extraordinary about the relationship between Margaret and myself. We were both young, it was war time and we filled each other's need for companionship. Our friendship, which could be characterised as young first love, was beyond reproach. We enjoyed walking and cycling together. Before dusk, after the evening meal, we would often take a long walk in a wooded park nearby. Sometimes, on my day off, we would bicycle to the foot of the Ringland Hills, taking along my portable radio. After parking our bikes, we would ascend the top of one of the slopes. There we would lay in the grass, listening to the American Armed Forces Radio music programs. Overhead the Eighth Air Force would be assembling, squadron after squadron, group after group, hundreds and hundreds of four-motor bombers creating a steady rumbling drone. From seeming confusion, would come order.

"Margaret's family often invited me to eat with them. I brought food from the base as much as I could. There was a vegetable garden in their back yard which supplemented their food. A storage shed was in a far corner. Her father told me he kept his plumbing tools in this shed during the German bombing blitz of 1941-42 in order to save them, in case a bomb destroyed his house. As fate would have it, no damage was ever done to their home, but a single incendiary bomb struck the shed, destroying most of his tools.

"The family could not help but laugh at my American style of eating. They would almost go into hysterics watching me pick up the fork with my right hand, the knife with my left then switch the knife to the right, fork to the left hand to (using their own words) 'jab at my meat' while I cut with my knife, then lay my knife down, switch the fork to my right hand and once more jab at my food.

"During the Blitz, Margaret's father had

bought a small piece of property approximately five miles north-east of Norwich. Up the slope, away from the river and close to the road, stood a small cabin. When the Luftwaffe was bombing the city, the family would cycle to this retreat. Many an afternoon, the whole family and I would cycle out to the camp. I rode the bike that they kept at the Red Cross in Norwich. Margaret's father almost had a fit when I told him I bought it for £50 ($250) from an airman who had completed his tour of duty. In today's coin, it would be like giving over a thousand dollars. I did have at least two of the three attributes the English credited to all Americans. I was over-paid and I was over there. Money meant nothing to me. One of the most relaxing activities I found was for Margaret and me to go rowing on the river. The current was very slow so that even rowing upstream required no real effort. The surface was so calm that it would seem as if it was a mirror. It was fun.

"One evening I left the family's house knowing that they planned to spend the following day at the river camp. I informed them that I had an early morning practice flight and to be on the look-out for my plane to overfly the camp. The next morning, I told pilots Peretti and Palmer what I wanted. They agreed that if I'd lead them to the site, they would fly low over the camp. As soon as I pointed out the exact building along the river bank, the pilots, revved the motors, getting them out of sync so they made a loud noise. I could see Margaret and the rest of the family standing in the yard waving at us. Then, Peretti did his thing. He banked to the right in order to recross the river, then turned back towards the cabin. Rather tall trees were about the building, but the camp site was in plain view. *Lili Marlene* headed straight towards the camp with the family still out in front, waving at us. We were diving straight at the cabin and trees, but at the last conceivable instant, Peretti and Palmer pulled up just in time. I saw Margaret's family throw themselves to the ground as they were sure it was all over for them.

"We returned to base in the early afternoon. As soon as I could, I caught the truck to town

1st Lieut John McLane Jr, on the right, with his crew's co-pilot, 2nd Lieut Burr Palmer, in front of the 68th Bomb Squadron combat crew quarters, *c.*1944.

and cycled to Margaret's family, arriving about supper time. Their eyes were still as big as saucers. We had given them either the biggest thrill in their lives or the worst fright. To this day I'm not sure which."

Aside from the relationships formed between American airmen and local girls, some of the most enduring friendships were forged between GIs and children living nearby the bases. There was, undoubtedly, an element of public relations involved, but it ran far deeper than that. As well as the frequent official parties staged for the benefit of war orphans and other local youngsters, many Americans, aircrews and ground crews, 'adopted' children, who were not only often more ready to accept their new transatlantic allies but were also happy to run errands in return for a few pennies and sweets. Many children came to idolise their American friends who, for their part, saw in the youngsters a reminder of home life and a welcome distraction from the stresses and strains of war. One such youngster, who became popular with Americans based at Attlebridge, was Eddie Brighty. In the accounts which follow, two former airmen and Brighty himself recall their days together.

James H.Lorenz arrived at Station 120, Attlebridge, home of the 466th BG, as a 20-year-old co-pilot and member of a B-24 replacement crew in 1944. As he settled into his officers' barrack building near the East gate, he began to learn some of the base customs: "Things like — if you wanted a good used bicycle — and this was a real need — you were to see 'Sgt So and So'. He would sell you one, 'used only on Sundays' by a departed crew, for a small fortune. One of the more fortunate options was that our barracks had their laundry done by an English lady, who lived just outside our base.

"This lady was Mrs Patience Brighty, whose family lived in Wood Farm Cottage, right outside the main gate. Doing 15-20 laundries gave her a tidy little income from these 'over-paid' Yanks and also provided a nice service for us. Her 12-year-old son, Eddie, picked up and delivered the laundry to our barracks.

"English youngsters were not normally allowed on the bases, but Eddie was not the average young brat. He was most shy, sincere and conscientious. And he appreciated all the chocolate, candy, fruit or gum we usually supplied him. He even liked 'K' rations! In return, his mother used to send along some fresh eggs for us twice a week — strictly forbidden by English rules, as they were rationed. But they were tasty!

"By some fast talking, we managed to get Eddie a special pass which allowed him to be on the base for our convenience, and he never once violated our trust in him or caused any problem."

As new crews arrived, young Eddie would be their first contact with the local population. Earl Wassom, then a B-24 pilot, remembers their initial meeting: "He came by our quarters, marched up to me, extended his hand and said, 'Hello, I am Eddie.'"

So impressed was Wassom's squadron commander with Eddie's friendly helpfulness, he issued him with a permanent pass which allowed him to pass through the guard station unchallenged on his way to the barracks.

Wassom adds: "True, he picked up our dirty laundry and his mother made it useful again, but Eddie was also our encourager. He always knew who was flying a mission. When the time approached for our return, he would build a fire in our little stove in the barracks to take away the chill. When a crew was lost in combat, he watched sadly as their belongings were gathered up by someone...He knew their fate before the next of kin were notified. He would get alone and cry — he had lost another American friend."

As a token of thanks, Wassom offered Eddie his choice of present for Christmas 1944. It turned out to be a bicycle bought from a shop in Norwich.

"As I delivered Eddie's gift, his eyes twinkled and his shy boyish smile melted our hearts. The glow on his face may have had something to do with the fog and scud disappearing from around

Eddie Brighty, a favourite with Americans at Attlebridge, with two model planes 'built from Norwich kits' and given him by an airman.

Attlebridge and all of East Anglia the next morning. For on Christmas Eve the largest air assault ever assembled delivered their Christmas loads of 'gifts' to assist our troops slugging it out in the Battle of the Bulge.

"That day, about 100 children from the area around Attlebridge were invited to a Christmas party at the Aero Club on base. The airmen were not present to attend the party since every 'flyable' aircraft and every crew was in the air. But Eddie was there, celebrating with the other children with a special shine on his face."

Eddie Brighty has never forgotten his wartime friends. He remains in contact with some, and the memories are never far away.

He recalls: "They always treated me so well. They were so good. It was as if I was their own child. I'd go on to the base straight out of school, and if they were out on a mission I'd light them

a fire for when they got back.

"Sometimes, it would be extremely painful, especially being so young. I remember once out of a hut for 30 men, only one crew returned. It was very saddening and I can remember crying my heart out on occasions.

"After a while, some of them insisted I got a job in the Officers' Club. I'd work there from 8am till 4.30pm. If there was a dance in the evening, they'd ask me to collect up glasses and bottles. I used to get £2 a week and £1 extra if I worked on a dance night. It was certainly good pay. When I started work in the city after the war, I was earning 17s 6d a week, and I had to pay 4s 9d for a weekly bus ticket out of that!"

Eddie is seen here again with Earl Wassom's crew at Attlebridge. Wassom is on the far left.

It was a photo call for the folks back home, but young Malcolm Holmes didn't mind. All he had to do was smile and tuck into a plateful of ice-cream. His house, at Eccles Heath, was virtually in the middle of the Snetterton base. He recalls: "They came along in a truck, took me to the mess for the photo which they told me was going in the American papers."

MAKING FRIENDS

Uncle Sam's youngest recruit? Little Geoffrey Holmes was barely four years old when he posed with his American friend at Snetterton, home of the 96th BG.

Joe Stryker and Rick Rokicki, who were based at Horsham St Faith with the 458th BG, found a home from home with the elderly Rolfe family who lived next to the airfield. They are seen here relaxing in the garden in Taylor's Lane, Old Catton, together with the Rolfes' widowed daughter, Florence Buck, and their grand-daughter Judith Rolfe. Now Mrs Miller, Judith recalls Americans visiting her school and adds: "We went to a party they organised at the base where I tasted ice-cream for the first time ...A Christmas tree was decorated entirely with 'Life-savers', a kind of fruit sweet with a hole in the middle rather like the modern 'Polo'. She has maintained contact with her American friends and at a reunion an ex-GI handed her a box of chocolates. He explained: "I gave you candy when I first met you as a little girl in 1943 and I have never forgotten the warmth and friendship shown to me when I was welcomed into your family."

Youngsters cluster around a returning 453rd BG crew at Old Buckenham on February 21, 1944. They include Pat Ramm, who had sewn the Top/Sergeant stripes, given to him by a Tibenham-based airman at Christmas 1943, to his overcoat.

A couple of unidentified Yanks pose with a group of local girls and their children in Castle Park, Thetford. The boy on the extreme left is Brian Fisher, who still lives in the town.

American airmen from Watton joined staff and children for the Carbrooke School Christmas party in 1944. Included here are the Revd George Chambers, centre of middle row, with headteacher, Miss Mary Norton, left centre, and teacher, Miss Eileen Sculfer.

There was an added touch of poignancy about this Anglo-American group at Seething. The young boy on the left, Norman Jermy, was destined to die as a child, while the airman with his hands on his shoulders, Bombardier Lieut Carroll 'Bud' Michaels, would be killed during a mission against Magdeburg. The others in the group are (back row, left to right): Lieut Frank P.Law, Lieut Jack Potgeter, Warrant Officer Jules Klingsburg and Lieut William Hammes; (front row) Dennis Lain, Bob Littlewood, Jimmy Saunders and his brother Ted. Law recalls the Christmas party of 1944 on the base: "All of the children were extremely well-behaved ...and, needless to say, it made the day such a memorable one for all of us ...We had a feast fit for a king ...We also had entertainment which included a moving picture and a visit from Santa Claus...The theatre was so crowded that most of us held our little guests on our laps."

Young George Waters, the laundry boy at Seething, became one of the best known characters among the airmen of the 448th BG. Edward T.Chu, a tail gunner from the 714th Squadron pictured here with him, recalls how one of the airmen had christened him 'Little 'arry 'awkins'. "He would pick up laundry, which his mother did at home. He was a likeable and easy going boy, and would be invited as a guest by the crew members at occasions like Christmas dinner at the combat mess. This was done by many other crews for other children...It was the least we felt we could do."

Children from West Lynn Primary School had a lesson with a difference when they visited Wendling airfield, home of the 392nd BG, in the late spring of 1944. They are seen here with their headmaster, Mr H.B.Fisher, and the USAAF officer is Capt Don MacLammond, of the 578th Squadron who acted as a public relations officer. The B-24 in the background, *Flying Patch*, flew 87 missions.

Bill O'Neil, a flight engineer and top turret gunner with the 453rd BG based at Old Buckenham, finds a four-legged friend in a Norwich park. One of his favourite haunts was the St Giles' Gate pub, and he recalls stopovers with the Sexton family next door.

A youngster destined to become one of the nation's most famous mothers was a special guest at this B-24 christening ceremony at Wendling on August 10, 1944. The girl, seen here second left, is the Hon Frances Roche, future mother of Princess Diana. With her sister, Mary, and father, the Harvard-educated Lord Fermoy, MP for King's Lynn, she saw *Birdie Schmidt*, the American Red Cross programme director for the enlisted men's club, smash a wrapped bottle of coke over the nose gun of the aircraft named after her. Birdie is on the left, alongside her nose art image, with 392nd BG CO, Lieut Col Lorin Johnson on the right. B-24 Birdie Schmidt flew 63 missions before being shot down during a raid on Magdeburg on February 15, 1945. Lord Fermoy, whose mother was American, had resigned a commission in the RAFVR after winning the Lynn by-election in 1943.

Sgt Wally Balzer, assistant to the base chaplain at Seething, was one of many Americans from the 448th BG befriended by the Mobbs family of Hedenham. He recalls: "Initially two GIs were invited to visit this family, but the number continued to grow as other fellows were added to those who found their home a friendly haven. Mrs Hilda Mobbs was the local postmistress ...Little Jennifer (seen here with Balzer) was an adopted child who was a bright light in this home. She celebrated her eighth birthday in September 1944, at which time some of us assisted her in celebration."

Memorable Flights

KENNETH Jewell was distinctly unimpressed by his new-found surroundings. With its clinging mud and biting winds that appeared to take no account of the seasons, Shipdham, in the depths of rural Norfolk, was definitely not a place for the faint-hearted.

"I don't believe I was ever really warm or without a cold the whole time we were there," he recalls. "And we never did get a shower or bath. When it rained hard, we stripped, ran outside and washed ourselves ...Life wasn't very pleasant."

The dank and dreary living quarters for the 66th Squadron, 44th Bomb Group, appeared every bit as bleak as the weather. In all, there were some 25 metal Nissen huts scattered across what had been a farmer's field. Each had a small coal stove, a single wash basin and, or so it seemed, its own family of rats. Bullet holes peppered the huts, evidence of the crude attempts to cull the rodent population with .45 automatics.

"We made a competitive game out of it," recalls Jewell. "If you got ten rat tails you were presented with a small metal mouse to pin on your clothes — five more tails got you a cheese cluster."

It was, as Jewell recalls, just about the best form of relaxation they had on the base outside of parties — and they, contrary to legend, were few and far between.

By the time he was transferred to the 66th at Shipdham, 1st Lieut Kenneth G. Jewell was already a combat veteran, having flown four missions with the 392nd BG out of Wendling. A bluff, plain-speaking Pennsylvanian with Indian blood coursing through his veins, he also had a reputation for run-ins with authority — the most notable occasion being in Tucson, Arizona, before heading over to England.

Having trained to fly B-17 Flying Fortresses, he was astonished to discover himself posted to a unit equipped with B-24 Liberators, derisively nicknamed the 'flying banana boat' on account of its unattractive bulbous shape.

Given his fiery temperament there could be only one response. "I refused to fly them," he recalls. That he changed his mind was due only to the threat of a court martial!

During the months that followed, Jewell and his crew of 'cast offs' and 'mavericks' would have cause to give thanks to the sturdiness and reliability of Consolidated's heavy bomber. "Out of 29 missions, we came back two times with all four engines operational; the rest we had three engines except for two when we only had two engines and once when we had one good engine and the other on fire..."

The last-mentioned mission was against the heavily-defended German port of Bremen.

Having pressed on to bomb the target despite the loss of one engine, Jewell's aircraft, the *Banshee*, was ambushed by fighters and raked by fire. Number two engine was blown apart, and almost immediately number one engine began belching flames and smoke. The damage inside the badly-hit bomber was no less severe.

Two headquarters officers, flying as observers, were fatally wounded, two crewmen injured, the main radio wrecked and the forward oxygen supply knocked out.

Jewell feathered the number two engine, but could do nothing to put out the fire in the number one engine. Losing altitude all the time, he took the gamble of pushing the only fully operational engine wide open. "We didn't care if it blew up," he records. "Every second in the air was closer to England." Emerging out of cloud, Jewell spotted another battle-scarred B-24. It was in a fearful state, an engine out, one wheel

1st Lieut Kenneth Jewell, second right in front row, with his crew in front of their aircraft in October 1943. They include, Lieut Matthew Foley, bombardier, far right, front row, Lieut Arthur Sakowski, third right, front row, and Stanislaus Lipcynski, radio operator, third right, back row. The *Banshee* pictured here crash-landed at Deopham Green on December 16, 1943.

hanging down and the body of a decapitated waist-gunner half in and half out of the fuselage. Then, the fighters came in again and the two bombers were separated.

Hit again, Jewell's aircraft escaped into cloud. "We were in bad shape," he recalls. "Someone, I believe it was the navigator, started the *Lord's Prayer* and soon everyone was repeating it."

Then, incredibly, the cloud opened and the sun hit the wounded *Banhsee*, melting the ice which had formed dangerously on the wings. Hopes rose again, but, with the aircraft losing altitude at roughly 400ft per minute, it appeared certain they would have to take their chances in the North Sea.

Only by throwing out all movable equipment, including parachutes, and the bodies of the two officers, who had succumbed to their injuries, did they gain sufficient height to limp back to Shipdham.

Even then, disaster was but narrowly avoided. As the *Banshee* came in low, she sliced off the tops of a line of trees and cut through the Control Tower antennae before ploughing sideways across the runway on to the grass.

"Up to this point," Jewell remembers, "I was calm and collected. Then, I began to shake, and so did my co-pilot.

We could not get out of our seats, we were so weak ...Some of the ground crew got us out and I began to sob ...Here I was, 21 years old, and the co-pilot and I had our hair turned grey. I was an old young man."

Their survival had been little short of miraculous. According to Jewell, on that day he was born again. "The tough crew I had were also changed," he says. "This terrible experience changed our outlook on life."

Harrowing as that mission was, however, it was to be eclipsed by events on March 9, 1944, when Jewell and his crew were given the honour of leading the second section of the 2nd Air Division's strike against an airframe factory in Brandenburg, near Berlin. The aircraft they flew that day was the *Banshee III*, and the story of that extraordinary mission is recounted in Jewell's own words:

"...we were awakened at 3am and taken to headquarters, where we were briefed on bomb-loading, fuel, armament, the route, take-off time, rendezvous time, height, time to head for Europe, bombing height, etc.

"Everything went smoothly over the Channel. We had good fighter cover and this continued all the way to the target. The flak over Europe was continuous and very heavy over Germany. We hit the turning point 15 seconds early and aimed for the target. The long line of bombers behind us were right in line. I lined up the bomber and set up the auto pilot for the bombardier. Lieut Matthew Foley was an excellent bombardier. The bombs were released and immediately the *Banshee* was hit severely by four bursts of flak. My leg struck me in the face. One engine was destroyed.

"Leaving on the auto pilot, the young, inexperienced co-pilot and I got the engine shut down. The engineer hollered in my ear, 'The oxygen is gone!' He gave us auxiliary bottles of oxygen which were good for six minutes. I tried the intercom and it was mute. Then, the navigator hit my shoulder and asked, 'Who's hit?' He knew it was someone on deck because of all the blood over his desk papers. 'The nose assembly and floor is done up front!' he yelled.

"The bombardier appeared beside him, saying, 'The nose gunner is stuck in the front turret with no floor!' I told him to get some straps and swing across and release the door and send him to the rear. All this, I understood, he did ...

"The navigator then told me to get out of the seat and he would patch me up. I adjusted the auto pilot on course for home and started losing altitude. I told the co-pilot to signal alternate lead to take command. He failed to do this, not knowing how without a radio, and could not find the Aldis lamp to signal him...

"When I tried to get up, to my surprise, I could not get out of my seat. Lieut Arthur Sakowski, an ex-football player and very strong, picked me up and laid me on the deck. He cut the pant-leg off, and it was a mess. Only the bicep muscle (of my left leg) was there. We had nothing to splint it, so he put sulphur on it and gave me two shots of morphine. Lieut Sakowski then tore the bottom of the seat from a parachute to get the jungle

knife. He then began to saw and hack at the remains of my leg, but the blade was too dull.

"I saw Lieut Foley, the bombardier, climb into my seat, and wondered why. The radio operator, Stanislaus K.Lipszynski, and engineer, William Wike, were dragging the co-pilot down beside me. He was unconscious. It seemed as though he could not stand the sight of blood, vomited in his oxygen mask and passed out. The bombardier and radio operator revived him. The guns started hammering away and I knew we were in trouble. I pulled myself up to a window and, to my surprise, the 66th Squadron was with us, and we were out of the main stream of bombers.

"I told Art, 'Put me back in the seat, and put a tourniquet on my leg.' I straightened the plane, which was still on auto pilot, and told Foley and Wike to keep an eye on things, and then I passed out.

"The next time I awakened, the co-pilot was in his seat and we were over the English Channel, losing altitude. I again put the plane under control, and passed out. When I awoke we were just above the balloon barrage in Norwich. We saw the field (Shipdham). Someone shot red flares and I headed for the runway. 'You handle the rudder,' I told the co-pilot. 'You handle the wheels and flaps,' I told the engineer. 'Everyone else,' I said, 'go back as far as you can. We will make it ride the skid...'

"We landed successfully, with nose high. When it slowed up, the nose was buried and I passed out. The next thing I knew, someone said, 'I'll get him', and I was picked up. The pain was terrible and I struck the person in the face ...I was lain on a stretcher and demanded to see the damaged *Banshee* before I got in the ambulance. I remember being wheeled into the operating room and the last words I heard were, 'We'll save you, Jewell'."

Unbeknown to Jewell at the time, those final desperate moments of the *Banshee's* perilous return to Shipdham were captured on film by a movie news crew, who had accompanied a group of high-ranking officers on a tour of the base. They had landed back at around 5.30pm — some

Shipdham, March 9, 1944. Following Lieut Jewell's extraordinary feat, the *Banshee III* lies nosed in after sliding to a halt.

five hours after Jewell had been hit. He was not operated on, however, until 1.30am, and for a simple reason:

"I was declared dead upon arrival at the hospital. They had so many wounded and so few doctors. When the doctor told an orderly to tie a tag on my toe, he ran and told him my toe twitched."

Jewell did not come round until the following afternoon: "My sides hurt so bad that I forgot about the leg. My bladder had not emptied itself in 30 hours. I filled three urinal ducts. I threw back the sheets and I had no left leg! I got furious, flung myself out of bed, tore off the bandages and started bleeding again. I could not accept the fact. I was young, had a good career, a beautiful wife and here I was to be a helpless cripple all my life."

In fact, Kenneth Jewell's life had barely begun. Astonishingly, he was flying again less than a year after his terrible injuries. Fitted out with an artificial leg, he resumed flying duties in February 1945, thanks to the support of General H.H.Hap Arnold, becoming the first member of the USAAF to fly with a wooden leg. Retiring as a much-decorated major in 1946, he went on to lead a full and active life, becoming a judge in his home state of Pennsylvania and the father of four children. He also carried on flying, having gained a commercial licence, until 1979.

His selfless heroism during that shattering mission to Berlin may possibly have been equalled, but seldom, if ever, surpassed. He received America's second highest gallantry award, the Distinguished Service Cross, an honour 'richly deserved' in the view of his flight engineer, Edward Guzik. But there were many who felt it should have been the highest award, including Brigadier-General Leon W.Johnson, who presented Jewell with his DSC as he lay, recovering, in hospital.

"He apologised to me," recalls Jewell. "He said he had personally recommended the Medal of Honor and could not understand the mix-up."

Out and About

Off duty. A group of 467th BG officers head out through the distinctive wrought-iron entrance to Sir Edward Stracey's estate next to Rackheath base famously remembered as the 'Golden Gates'. The gateway served as the entrance on to the road in to Norwich, the main destination for 'liberty runs'.

One of the first ports of call for members of the USAAF visiting Norwich was the historic Bishop's Palace which was officially opened as the American Red Cross Services Club on July 10, 1943. Established as a leave hostel, the building near the Cathedral became a focal point for American airmen. One room was converted into a caféteria, and on the eve of the opening the *EDP* reported: "They have equipped many rooms as dormitories, installed dozens of showers, which Americans prefer to baths, and transformed the ancient vaulted kitchen with rows of modern cooking and refrigerating apparatus." State nights were to be staged each week, regular entertainment laid on, garden parties organised in the Palace grounds and outings arranged to visit the Broads.

A party of Americans are swallowed up in the shadow of the buildings in front of the majestic Cathedral which figured high on the sightseeing tour. Note the air-raid shelter on the left.

Captain Howard Adams, a pilot with the Shipdham-based 44th BG, visited the city for the first time on October 17, 1942, just a week after his squadron arrived in Norfolk. In his diary, he recorded: "Our first impression of Norwich ...was the numerous buildings that had been blasted by bombs or gutted by fire. Several churches, one railroad station, and many stores and apartment houses had been reduced to shambles. The Germans used Norwich for target practice back in '40 and '41 *(but primarily during the so-called Baedeker blitz of April 1942. Author's note)* and still it is occasionally bombed. After searching for several hours for a place to stay, we finally found a small shabby hotel of an ancient vintage that had rooms of a sort ...We then went over to the Royal Hotel for dinner of fillet sole which was good but not much to get fat on. After strolling the streets a bit we went to a dance at the Samson and Hercules Inn. Scotch soldiers in their kilts, British soldiers and sailors, WAAFs, and many US officers and men filled the dance hall. Everyone danced the peculiar windmill sort of dancing. After the dance we were so tired we went to bed, to ride back to Thurston in a taxi ...we got our bikes and struggled the rest of the way back to the field, tired and exhausted."

Howard Adams died on February 26, 1943, when his bomber was shot down by German fighters during a raid on Bremen. He was 25 years of age.

The coastal resorts of Yarmouth and Lowestoft were popular with Americans on leave from their bases. Here, Capts Robert Tienken, 350th Squadron adjutant, and Frank Seibert, the squadron mess officer, from Thorpe Abbotts, are preparing for a swim at Lowestoft in 1944. Note the barbed wire barricades, reminders of the invasion scare four years earlier.

Fish and chips quickly became a favourite meal for Americans on leave from their bases. Here, S/Sgt Bob Einheuser, from the 448th BG, and a cousin, Bud Wisman, from the 44th BG, tuck in beside a Norwich bomb site in 1944.

Waiting for the bus. A GI stands with his girlfriend beside the signpost at Poringland.

Some Americans found their relaxation by messing about in boats on the Broads. Here two members of the 448th BG from Seething put their sailing skills to the test.

Anyone for cricket? Somewhere in Norfolk, members of the Snetterton-based 96th BG foresook their baseball bats to join in that traditional English summer sport.

Pubbing

Pubbing, as they called it, became probably the main recreation for American airmen out to enjoy a few off-duty hours. Every base had its favourite locals. And despite their running joke about Britain's warm beer, many young Americans formed lasting attachments to the pubs that offered them precious diversions from the hardships and horrors of war.

Jim Gregory was one of a small group of airmen from the 467th BG, based at Rackheath, who made the Jolly Butchers pub their own 'home away from home.' He recalls: "It would never occur to us to go anywhere else. The proprietress was a lady we called Annie (I never did know her last name). Annie was the focal point of the evening. She sang like a gravel-voiced nightingale. Her rendition of *Ragged But Right* is still the best I have ever heard. Once a week she found ice, where I don't know, and iced down bottles of ale for her American guests. When one of us failed to return from a mission, she shed our tears and the bond between us grew stronger. I recall a 'regular' who was involved in a crash on take-off one morning. They found him wandering in a field outside the base, badly burned. I went to see him in the hospital that afternoon. He was bandaged from head to toe with slits for his eyes and mouth. As I leaned over him,

he whispered 'Tell Annie I won't be there tonight'. Such was our love for the lady and her pub."

Men of the 448th BG based at Seething could choose between the Mermaid, the Tumble Down Dick and the Cherry Tree. Given the reliance on two-wheeled transport, the airmen frequently adopted the watering hole closest to them.

William Bullard, who flew with the 713th Squadron, recalls: "The pub our crew most frequently used and called our own was the Mermaid (or the Swinging Teat) ...It was located a short bicycle ride from the back entrance to the base. The bicycle rides back to the base ...usually consisted of members of the same crew riding in a group, joined in song at the top of their lusty, Yank voices. On one occasion, this practice almost proved disastrous to our unit. As was common, our return to base was well after nightfall and, what with our singing most likely very much off key and the blackout, a military

Ethel Riches, landlady of the Royal Standard in Shipdham, became something of a surrogate mother for a succession of young airmen from the 44th BG. As a thank you, they threw a party for her on the base. While the Royal Standard was mainly frequented by officers, the men preferred the King Billy (King William) on the corner of the airfield.

A party from the Seething base pose with a couple of locals outside the Mermaid pub.

The sign which gave the pub its nickname.

convoy also observing blackout almost ran the lot of us over. Had it been visible to them I am quite certain the drivers of those vehicles would, to this day, be in stitches at our mad scramble to clear the roadway..."

Carl Wunderlich, of the 58th Station Complement Squadron, was another Mermaid regular. His abiding memory was of the landlady, Mrs Barker, calling "Time, ladies and gentlemen, please", while a GI pal played the piano in another room 'with everyone gathering around singing'.

Bloomin' Snowdrops

With their distinctive white belts, gaiters, clubs, first-aid pouches and, of course, helmets, the American Military Police, otherwise known as the 'Snowdrops', became a familiar sight on the streets of Norfolk during the latter half of the war. Their nickname, however, was somewhat misleading. They were not beyond employing strong-arm methods to enforce the law and fully lived up to their unofficial motto: 'Aggressive in offense'.

Primarily tasked with ensuring order was maintained by off-duty airmen venturing into Norwich and the villages surrounding their bases, they patrolled on foot and in jeeps around pubs and nightclubs.

The 'Snowdrops' belonged to the 987th MP Company, a unit of the 8th USAAF, which arrived in Norwich in January 1943. Originally billeted at Horsham St Faith base, they were eventually quartered in private homes along Lower Clarence Road and Rosary Road, Norwich.

Their main 'response centre' was the old Plough Inn, on the corner of Market and Farmers Avenue. Brad Cain, who had been a City of Boston police officer before becoming an MP, recalls: "We used the bar as the front desk. People could come in and make a complaint or request …A number of men were ready to respond to a 'shout' at all times. A response jeep would often be parked outside, ready for action."

As the USAAF in Norfolk grew so did the work of the MPs. Another Company was absorbed into the 987th, and detachments were assigned to King's Lynn, Yarmouth and Morley, where the 231st Station Hospital was located. At its peak the Company numbered around 350 men and included its own CID unit. Inevitably, those MPs serving in the city and larger towns, with a greater number of dance halls and pubs,

Snowdrops, together with their senior officers, line up with their Norwich police counterparts.

were kept busiest. On one occasion a fight broke out, near The Bell pub, in the centre of Norwich, between Americans and Scottish soldiers, who didn't take kindly to jokes about their kilts. Redcaps — British MPs — and Snowdrops were quickly on the scene. Cain remembers: "The Redcaps and local police went for the British and we weeded out the Americans. A local policeman tried to intervene and instruct one of my MPs to arrest a GI. In the confusion, the MP clubbed him over the head and knocked him out as well. The Chief Constable requested an apology from the Army Air Force police..."

Life was generally easier out in the countryside. John Rex served with Detachment 'B', based at Morley. His patrol patch included Dereham, Bungay and Wymondham. Trouble, he recalls, was the exception rather than the rule: "The American soldier, who spent off-duty time in the villages, was there because he enjoyed the friendly atmosphere and camaraderie he found in the 'local'.

"For a couple of months prior to D-Day we

Snowdrops jeep patrol through East Harling in 1944. Included among the MPs is John Rex, on the right at the rear.

had serious racial problems in the village of East Harling, and for nearly all of my 2½ year service in Norfolk we had periodic problems with itinerant farmworkers."

The Carrow Road stadium on November 30, 1944, was the venue for a parade of the Norfolk-based 987th MP Company, with Detachment B from Morley leading the way.

Ride 'Em Cowboy

IT WAS the day the Wild West came way out east. The Grand Rodeo staged at Carrow Road — the home of Norwich City Football Club — on August 7, 1943, proved a big hit with a local populace weaned on western movies.

Around 6,000 people paid prices ranging from 5s 0d (25p) for the best seats in the stands to 1s 0d (5p) on the terraces to watch the extraordinary spectacle. Among the crowd were many youngsters who took advantage of a half-price offer to see what the *EDP* described as 'something of the romance of a Texan ranch' in the heart of Norfolk.

The event was the highlight of Norfolk and Norwich Charities Week and helped lift an otherwise flagging fund-raising appeal to fresh heights.

Organised by Lieut Jocko Maher of the USAAF, a former Texas Rough Rider and, according to the advertising bills, a 'film star', the rodeo boasted 'riders from the southern and western states of the USA' — all drawn from the air bases ringing the city.

The result was a triumph as memorable as any in Carrow Road's proud sporting history. The *EDP* reported: 'The absence of wide-brimmed hats and other conventional accessories of cowboy costumes was more than compensated for by the skill of the performers.'

The same account went on: 'Galloping, leaping, lassoing their way about, and accompanied by the weird yodellings of *'Ragtime Annie'* and *'Cowboy Sweetheart'*, aided by a Hill Billy Band, these American soldier-cowboys, with Lieut Maher as ring master, performed many feats of reckless but expert horsemanship.'

Ride 'em cowboy …a bare-back rider bolts out of the pen at Carrow Road's River End.

It was a case of riding by the 'seat of your pants' as the steers took centre stage.

Among the highlights of an action-packed programme that included steer riding, bucking horses and bare-back relays were attempts to milk a wild cow, a 'catch the greased pig' competition and yodelling solo by Sgt Gene Radcliffe, better known as 'Montana Slim'.

Lighting up time for the rodeo fire-eating display.

By 1943, the Americans were beginning to take the strain in the Grand Alliance, but surely this was going a bit far...

American servicemen mingle with civic dignatories and an enthralled crowd of spectators in the old wooden Main Stand which was destroyed by fire 41 years later. The man with the microphone, sandwiched between the Stars and Stripes and the Union Flag, could be Captain Pat Larsen, of Iowa, the rodeo commentator.

Youngsters found a variety of vantage points to watch their new-found American friends perform — including a ranch-style fence complete with ladder!

Memorable Flights

THE Dutch aviation researchers were baffled and more than a little perplexed by the mysterious crash of a Norfolk-based Liberator near the little village of Hagenstein almost 50 years earlier. They had traced the identity of the bomber and eyewitnesses had described its gentle 'emergency landing'. But there was something strange about the fate of B-24J 42-50566 which puzzled them.

First, they could trace no record of any crew members and second, there was the curious timing of the crash. It had occurred at 11.05pm, surprisingly late given that the 8th Air Force was flying daylight operations.

The solution when it came was as extraordinary as the puzzle itself...

August 2, 1944. Captain Kenneth Madden's 448th BG crew had been assigned a veteran B-24, christened *Bar Fly*, for the 'two-bit' raid on oil storage tanks at Pacy-sur-Armance in France. But at the last-minute mechanical troubles forced them to switch to a spanking new ship. B-24J 42-50566 had flown only two missions.

Compared with raids deep into Germany, it had all the makings of an 'easy mission', and it appeared to be working out that way as Madden led the 12-plane lower left squadron in towards the target. There was some confusion as they turned to head for home, but the formation had sorted itself out by the time they approached the French coast.

It was then, however, that they ran into trouble. Lieut Jack Werts, the bombardier, recalled: "Apparently we flew over a mobile flak battery, and those German boys could shoot. One, two, three, four flak bursts exploded right under the airplane, with the bursts coming at about two-second intervals. There were audible 'splats' of fragments hitting the plane after each burst. Most surely had we not finally gotten out of range, a fifth burst would have knocked us out of the air."

Just how close they had come to disaster was only revealed when the aircraft crossed the English coast and Werts and the engineer, Sgt Vernon Robertson, made a tour of the damage. The aircraft resembled a flying sieve. Six-inch holes had been punched in the bomb bay, a larger one was torn in the wing-tip, the hydraulic system had been hit and the empty 'Tokyo' fuel tank shot out of the starboard wing. It was a miracle that none of the crew had been injured.

Their troubles, however, were far from over. By the time they were over Seething, the cloud base was no more than 400ft from the ground. Only then, did they discover the wheels could not be lowered. In his diary, co-pilot, Lieut Frank Lyden recorded what happened next: "We went back up through the 'soup' where we could try our emergency procedures without worrying about the hundreds of other ships trying to get on the ground. In our first attempt to lower the gear, we about lost all the fluid in the system.

"Trying to crank them down by hand, 'Muscles' Werts snapped the cable which, evidently, had been damaged. We now had no wheels, no flaps, no brakes and not enough gas to reach the nearest crash-landing field with the weather the way it was. We informed the tower of the situation and the Colonel, bless him, got on the air and ordered Ken to bail out all but the pilot and co-pilot. We figured that he wanted us to crash-land, but when the other boys had left, he ordered us to head the ship toward the Fatherland and hit the silk ourselves.

"I remember the surprise I felt with the terrific 'swish' of the slip-stream and then the comparative silence with only the wind whistling by my ears as I fell away from the ship. It was easy to gather my scattered marbles. It was so quiet and peaceful floating down. I was on my

Captain Kenneth Madden's regular crew. They were joined by an extra gunner for the mission of August 2, 1944. The full crew that day was: pilot, Capt Kenneth Madden; co-pilot, Lieut Frank Lyden; navigator, Lieut George J.Peterson; bombardier, Lieut Jack Werts; engineer, Sgt Vernon Robertson; radio operator, Sgt Peter B.Lewis; top turret, Sgt Fred Kerniss; nose gunner, Sgt Richard Bernaud; tail gunner, Sgt Daniel J.Kramer; waist gunner, M.D.McLendon.

back and in good spirits, so I thought I might try to control my fall by spreading my arms. As I did my body began to spin; head-first on my back, still. It all happened in a matter of ten seconds, and when I started to spin I looked down at the 'D' ring, held my breath and pulled. Because of my altitude, the jolt of the 'chute opening was a little rough and I must have hit myself in the mouth 'cause I had a fat lip when I picked myself up after a comparatively easy landing.

"On the way down, I saw Ken doing OK. I waved to him but he was a good quarter mile away and didn't notice it. As I went into the clouds the droning of a ship coming towards me gave me some anxious moments but it passed on by below. I broke out on a peaceful country scene; a farmhouse, road and fields and before I had a chance to pick my landing place I hit pretty hard but comfortably, a thankful, happy boy."

All ten crew members had exited safely and come down close to Hardwick. Of their faithful B-24, however, nothing more was known. It was simply assumed she had gone down over the sea. Writing in his diary directly after the mission, Lyden noted: "The only thing we regret is that

we didn't get the chance to count the holes in poor, shot-up 566. Maybe it's best we don't know."

What neither Lyden nor any other member of the crew knew then, or for many years afterwards, was that their grievously damaged B-24, set to fly on auto-pilot, had not merely reached the North Sea — it had crossed over it. Making its landfall somewhere along the Dutch coast, it had somehow evaded the German defences before its fuel tanks ran dry near the village of Hagenstein.

The rest of the story was related by aviation researcher John A.Hey 49 years later: "The B-24 came down gliding, hit three pollard-willows lined along a ditch, skidded into a meadow, killing 15 cows. The wreckage was removed by German pioneers some days later…"

Despite being, in the words of Jack Werts, 'damaged from cockpit to tail', the aircraft's final descent had been so smooth that it did not break up on impact. According to Hey: "No parts of the B-24 penetrated into the marshy ground." The mystery of Hagenstein's empty Liberator had finally been laid to rest.

Party Spirits

MAINTAINING morale has always been an important factor for military forces — and that was particularly true for any unit fighting far from home. The Americans understood this better than most. As well as their official touring entertainers from the USO, each base formed bands, singing groups and staged their own shows.

There were celebrations to mark milestones in the history of each group, such as 100 and 200 mission parties. There were annual Thanksgiving and Christmas festivities when hundreds of local children were shipped on to the bases. And there were, of course, the regular dances which drew local girls from the surrounding towns and villages, ferried in aboard the so-called 'passion wagons' or 'liberty buses'.

American dance styles and music, already popular in some quarters, quickly became the order of the day in village halls and the big dance halls. Station bands, many of them imitators of the Glenn Miller swing style, were allowed to play at charitable and commercial dances, all in the name of harmonious Anglo-American relations.

One of the earliest such bands was called the 'Jivin' Yanks', a seven-strong group of airmen led by Cpl Tony Pellegrino, who had arrived in Norfolk with the 8th Air Force by way of the fashionable clubs of Long Island. They helped make the dance in aid of the Drayton 'Wings for Victory' campaign go with a zing in May 1943, causing a degree of embarrassment in the process.

"I will not attempt a precise description of that strange word 'jive'," wrote a local newspaper reporter. "I gather, however, that it indicates jazz in its most modern and energetic forms." And he concluded: "I rather fancy that we will be hearing a good deal more of the 'Jivin' Yanks' in the future."

The 448th BG band, based at Seething, with accordion player George Dupont, second left on the back row, played at venues all over Norfolk between 1943 and 1945, including the Winter Gardens in Yarmouth.

Local girls mingle with American airmen at a squadron party on Shipdham air base in March 1944. The show was laid on by USO entertainers.

Men of the 389th BG mark Christmas at Hethel with a party of their own and a celebratory snapshot around the Christmas tree.

Christmas was as special for local children as it was for the Americans, many of whom donated their candy rations towards the annual festive parties laid on around the bases. Hearty meals were eaten, games played and presents handed out, usually by an airman clad in a Santa Claus costume. This celebration was held at Hardwick by members of the 93rd BG and the Red Cross on December 23, 1943.

Among the most popular touring troupes on the 2nd Air Division circuit was led by Major Newton McLaughlin. He is seen here, centre left, at one of his shows staged at Attlebridge.

One of the biggest and most memorable Christmas parties was staged by the 453rd BG at Old Buckenham in 1944. In all, some 1,250 children, aged from four to 14 and including orphans and evacuees, crowded on to the base to be entertained by a magician, to watch cartoons and be given stockings filled with candy and toys. Unusually, the celebrations were designed as much to help the children of recently-liberated Paris as much as give local youngsters a

good time. An appeal for toys produced a huge response and a crowd of children gathered around the appropriately-christened *Liberty Run*, complete with Santa Claus nose art, to autograph the aircraft and deliver their gifts. These were to be flown over to Paris aboard the B-24, with a French-speaking crew at the controls. Things did not quite go according to plan. On take-off, the aircraft slipped off the runway, and had to delay the trip until the following day.

Liberty Run, having another autograph added to its collection.

Chorus girls in full cry at Seething.

The cast of *It's All Yours, Buddy,* a 2nd Air Division talent show that toured many of the Norfolk bases.

The lavishness of the food and drink spreads laid on at the major base parties were sometimes as enticing to ration-fed locals as the airmen themselves. These two photographs show girls at Snetterton Heath air base in 1944 for the 96th BG's 250th mission party.

General Jimmy Doolittle, famed as the man who led the first raid on Tokyo in 1942, caught in unfamiliar pose with an ice-cream during the 100th BG's 200th mission party at Thorpe Abbotts on September 30, 1944. The base had acquired the ice-cream machinery from a Norwich business which had closed down for the duration of the war. Evidently, it was sold on the basis that the Americans would give the firm first refusal to buy their old equipment back at the end of the war.

Getting in the swing at an Officers' Club dance at Seething held to celebrate the 448th BG's 100th mission on June 24, 1944.

A variety of dance styles are displayed at Watton, where the men of the 3rd Strategic Air Depot were based.

Gable's Gaitors was the band of the 231st Station Hospital at Morley and took its name from their CO, Lieut Col Linwood M.Gable. What started out as a six-piece band grew to become one of the most famous among all those operating in England. The Gaitors, seen here on October 14, 1944 at a party to mark the 231st's first anniversary in Europe, performed on and off the base, broadcast on the British Forces Network and were invited to join the legendary Glenn Miller ETO orchestra for a concert at a nearby base. Led by pianist S/Sgt Harry Miller, they were reckoned to have been Lieut Col Gable's pride and joy. It was even said that Gable had traded two Chinese cooks to obtain Harry Miller's services. The band had the distinction of performing to crowds of revellers who swarmed outside the Rainbow Corner Red Cross Club in Piccadilly when first news of the imminent German surrender spread on May 7. *Yank Magazine* reported how the band 'moved out to the balcony and serenaded the mixed Allied crowd milling around on Shaftesbury Avenue'. And it added: 'Although it was almost impossible to move, jitterbugs and oldsters took the cue and danced as long as there was music.'

The Century Bombers, band of the 100th BG at Thorpe Abbotts, with an apt backdrop of a B-17 in one of the clubs on the base. The trombone and uniform belonging to Irv Waterbury, third left, front row, are now displayed in the 100th BG Control Tower Museum.

Edie Delainie was a well-travelled entertainer on the USO circuit and had the badges to prove it. This photograph was taken during a visit to Old Buckenham in company with Ella Logan.

In the Mood

OF ALL the great wartime big bands there was one which was to become synonymous with the days when the fields of Norfolk were turned into a 'Little America': the Glenn Miller band.

Even half a century later, his signature tune *Moonlight Serenade* and a host of other popular hits from *Little Brown Jug* to *Chattanooga-Choo-Choo* instantly evoke those GI years.

Miller himself arrived in Britain shortly after D-Day, with what would become known as the American Band of the Allied Expeditionary Force. During the previous year, the 40-piece ensemble had raised millions of dollars for the war effort in the States with a series of concerts at War Bond Rallies as well as supporting recruiting drives.

Their arrival in Britain, however, brought the USAAF's top bandleader in contact with a new army of fans: the vast number of American airmen bent on carrying the war into the heart of Germany and the British civilians who lived and worked near the bases.

Billeted at Bedford, Miller, accompanied by either his full orchestra or ensembles, began a mammoth list of engagements during the summer of 1944 which included a mini-tour of the 8th Air Force's Norfolk bases. Miller's first stop in the county was at Attlebridge on August 18, a day which also saw him and his dance band appear at the Samson and Hercules in Norwich. A week later, the orchestra performed at Wendling. It was followed by visits to Tibenham and Thorpe Abbotts on September 1, and Hardwick on September 12.

The pictures which appear here were taken when Miller and his dance band ensemble staged a memorable performance at Thorpe Abbotts, home of the 100th BG.

An audience of about 2,000 airmen from three bases and two hospitals packed Hangar No.2 at Thorpe Abbotts on September 1, 1944 for the Glenn Miller concert staged to celebrate the end of the 8th Air Force War Bond Drive.

Miller in full swing. The concert lasted 1½hrs and proved a huge success.

The world-famous AEF Band included some of the finest instrumentalists from the big band era with such names as Ray McKinley, Mel Powell, Michael 'Peanuts' Hucko and Trigger Alpert.

Glenn Miller, left, with an American Red Cross worker and, second right, Col Tom S.Jeffrey, CO of the 100th BG.

With the Miller band looking on, Capt Henry L.Hollingsworth Jr makes the War Bond draw with the help of one of the nurses on the base.

First and Last

OF ALL the missions undertaken by combat crews, the most significant, if not always the most dramatic, were often the first and, if they were lucky enough to survive, the last of their tour.

The first mission was something of a journey into the unknown, nervously yet eagerly awaited, a chance at last to put all their training to the test. By the time most crews reached their last mission there was generally only a desire to get it over with and to get home.

At the beginning of the USAAF bombing campaign, a tour consisted of 25 missions, but as the war progressed this figure stretched first to 30 and then to 35. Early on, however, losses were so heavy there was talk of reducing the number to 15 in order to give crews a realistic chance of survival.

In this chapter the stories of a first and a final mission are told by two airmen. Their accounts, based on their wartime diaries, present a vivid insight into the heady psychological mix of trauma and elation that bomber crews endured...

It was the autumn of 1944 when Sgt Kenneth R.Berkheimer arrived at Deopham Green to begin his tour with the 452nd Bombardment Group. An air gunner, he was a member of 1st Lieut Henry Bauer's crew. Conditions at Deopham were basic and, although combat crews had the best of the food on offer, it frequently left much to be desired. Before mission briefings, crews were sometimes treated to fresh egg omelettes, but mostly they were made from powdered eggs with grated cheese to make them edible.

In his graphic account of his wartime career, *Combat Story of The High Blower Crew*, Berkheimer relates: "On our first mission I don't remember anything I ate. Whatever it was it had all turned into a 'rolled up set of snow chains' in my stomach by the time the briefing officer raised the curtain on the 'target for today'. Everyone had sweaty palms..."

That first mission was to Meresburg, in Germany, on November 21, 1944. The target was a synthetic oil refinery. In his combat record, he wrote: "Anti-aircraft flak very heavy but inaccurate due to the multi-layered clouds. There were reported to be over 1,000 88mm guns located there to protect the industry in that area. Bombing results were good but we did not destroy the essentials of the synthetic refinery ...German fighters attacked the bomber line outside of Halle. Our group was not attacked although fighter contrails were all about us for the last 100 miles to the target.

"Our crew was totally exhausted when we returned. We all decided this war is 'hell'. We had an old, war weary B-17 airplane, full of patches and, although it had new engines, our pilots, Lieuts Bauer and Caldwell, had a lot of trouble staying in formation. You could quickly be a victim of the GAF (German Air Force) if you fell behind, so the tension on board was unbearable. We were not experienced enough to know what to really fear — and, believe me, there was plenty of fear to last on that first mission. It turned out we had burned the new engines so badly we could not stay in formation on the return..."

Ken Berkheimer went on to complete 34 missions, flying his last raid on March 26, 1945. He ended his combat career with six oak-leaf clusters to his Air Medal.

S/Sgt B.Dale Bottoms, a Texan, was assistant engineer in Crew 55, part of the 714th Bomb Squadron flying with the 448th BG out of Seething.

By June 1944, Bottoms and his crew were counting down towards their final mission. But rumours were rife that the tour would be stretched beyond 30 missions, and the strain was beginning to tell.

In his diary entry for June 16, he complained: "Well, the crazy fools expect us now to fly until ...well, God knows when..."

His next mission, his 29th, was one of the roughest of all. With their B-24 riddled by flak

Crew 55, 714th Squadron. Back row (left to right): Harold Smith, navigator; Bob Bettcher, co-pilot; Tom Keene, pilot; Ed Moran, bombardier; centre row: B.Dale Bottoms, asst. engineer and gunner; Grover Bingham, engineer; Chas Blanton, waist gunner; George Sansburn, tail gunner; bottom row: Fred Krepser, ball turret gunner; William Demetropoulos, radio operator.

Tour completed. The elation of finishing 30 missions was evident at Shipdham on May 9, 1944, when pilot Charles 'Chuck' Arnold, of the 66th Bomb Squadron brought B-24 *42-99967, Myrtle the Fertile* at zero height to beat up the strip.

over the target, an oil refinery at Politz, the crew were given the chance to head for neutral Sweden.

"We could go there and be interned for the rest of the war, but we wished to go home," wrote Bottoms.

Having ejected any loose equipment, they limped home to find no fewer than 200 flak holes in their aircraft. One piece of shrapnel tore through Bottoms' flying suit without touching him. Two days later, they set off for Guyancourt in France on their 30th and what would prove to

On this 2nd. day of Nov. nineteen hundred and forty four the fickle finger of Fate has traced on the rolls of the

LUCKY BASTARD CLUB

The Name of

ALBERT J. DEXTER JR., 0687682 1st. Lieut., Air Corps

Who on this date achieved the remarkable record of having sallied forth, and returned, no fewer than thirty times bearing tons and tons of high explosive Goodwill to the Feuhrer and would-be Feuhrers, through the courtesy of the Eighth Air Force A.A.F., who sponsors these programs in the interest of Government "of the people, by the people, and for the people."

COMMANDING OFFICER

AIR EXECUTIVE   SQUADRON COMMANDER

GROUP OPERATIONS OFFICER   GROUND EXECUTIVE

The message on the certificate says it all for 1st Lieut Al Dexter, of the Hethel-based 389th BG.

be, despite rumours to the contrary, their last raid in the ETO.

His exhilaration at completing his tour was reflected in his diary entry for June 22: "Well, I thank Thee Dear Lord! I thank the Almighty God for going with and protecting us throughout our tour and seeing us safely through. I will tell anyone that He is the best friend a guy can have. If it were not for God's help we would never have finished.

"We made our last mission and believe me we are a bunch of happy fellows. All of us except Bing (one of his original crew) finished today. We took off at 16.30 this afternoon, formed over England and headed out. We climbed on course, leading the group. We arrived at our target, an airfield in the outskirts of Paris at 19.14, dropped our bombs and returned to the base at 21.10.

"As we crossed the field, Capt Keene (pilot) told us to shoot off all the flares on board. That we did, as the ground crew saw that we had plenty guns and flares. It wasn't too bad. We did see some flak over the target, but God was with us and we made it okay. We have made it. Capt Keene told us in Herrington, Kansas, that he was going to carry us over there, make our tour and bring us back, so with God's help, he is going to do it. He is a great guy.

"All around we have a darn good crew. Capt Keene, a big guy, always flashing that moustache. Lieut Bettcher, co-pilot, a kid always smiling, a very nice guy. 1st Lieut Smith, nav, 'Relief tube Smitty' we called him. Darn good navigator. 1st Lieut Moran, bombardier, Mo. A regular GI. T/Sgt Bingham. Bing, an old worn-out honest-to-goodness engineer. Demo the Greek.

T/Sgt Demetropoulos, radio and boy what a kid. S/Sgt Krepser, ball and nose gunner. The kid from Galveston. Well 'Actung'. S/Sgt Sansburn, tail gunner. Well George is a good guy, but sad sack. Ha! And S/Sgt Blanton, 'Pappy'. Well, I am sorry to say he had not the pleasure of finishing with us. He went with another crew. He went down with them when they got shot down. We all mourned our loss. Pappy, a good man.

"That covers all except yours truly. I thank the Good Lord for going with us and helping us to be the best crew in the squadron and group. God help us to return home soon. We are to go over to the officer's barrack for a little get together tonight."

1st Lieut Leroy L.Engdahl made history at Seething on May 11, 1944, by becoming the first member of the original 448th BG to safely finish his 30 allotted missions. His return to base was the signal for a memorable 'fancy dress' celebration. After Base Commander Col Gerry Mason had congratulated him, his friends swiftly stripped him of his flying suit and dressed him in red, white and blue striped pyjamas, top hat and a giant replica DFC ribbon. Later, more formal celebrations took place with a special dinner held in honour of the 713th Squadron pilot. Engdahl's achievement was a great morale boost for a Group which had suffered severely, losing 75 planes in combat or as a result of accidents. He had flown 15 of his missions as a co-pilot and the remainder as a first pilot.

As a pilot without a regular crew, he had volunteered, save when ill or exhausted, to fly all missions until he finished his tour, and that included two missions in a single day. In all, he flew 13 different B-24s and on 26 of the 30 missions, including the last one aboard *Little Joe*, his aircraft had sustained damage. His narrowest escape came on February 5, 1944, during a raid on Tours when a Focke Wulf 190 shot a huge hole in the wing of his B-24.

"We were most fortunate our plane did not blow up then and also lucky in our pre-planned strategy on our landing, anticipating that the left landing gear was blown, we prepared accordingly and landed safely with the Lord's help. Many planes looked worse ...but it was a miracle we didn't explode as we were hit."

Nearly 40 years later Leroy Engdahl was elected vice-president of the 448th Group Veterans' Association and spearheaded a fund-raising appeal to renovate Station 146 Control Tower as a living memorial to the men who flew out of Seething.

Stars and Stripes

IT WAS Hollywood's own contribution to the war effort. As the conflict rolled remorselessly on, America's greatest stars were mobilised for morale-boosting tours of bases all over the world. Every Nissen hut was plastered with pin-ups — of which those of Betty Grable and Rita Hayworth figured most prominently — but nothing could compare with the personal appearances of celebrities whose very presence provided a rare release from the relentless grind of war. Throughout the war's duration, a steady succession of film stars, singers and musicians found their way on to the USAAF bases scattered across the Norfolk countryside. They were joined by celebrities, politicians and sportsmen, all hoping to provide a tonic for the troops!

Scarves were the order of the day when the legendary Marlene Dietrich made a flying visit to Watton, home of the 3rd Strategic Air Depot and 25th BG, in 1944. Dietrich, seen here with Col Leon Gray, later remarked: "The war gave me the opportunity of kissing more soldiers than any other person in the world." She was one of the most tireless of wartime entertainers, a fact recognised by the award of the Medal of Freedom, America's highest civilian honour, for her efforts to 'bring pleasure and cheer to more than 500,000 American soldiers.'

Hollywood tough guy James Cagney made an appearance at Hethel air base on March 30, 1944. The star, who made his name in a whole host of gangster roles during the 1930s, had enjoyed a huge success two years earlier in the musical biopic *Yankee Doodle Dandy*. His Oscar-winning portrayal of patriotic songwriter George M.Cohan was a masterpiece of flag-waving cinema. He is seen at Hethel reproducing his own unique style of tap dancing for which that film was remembered and posing with (left to right), entertainments officer Frank Rutledge, Lieut Edwards, the squadron commander, Lieut Col Philip Ardery and 389th BG CO, Lieut Col Robert B.Miller.

Clark Gable was at the height of his fame when World War Two broke out in 1939 — the same year that *Gone With The Wind* was released. Like James Stewart, he joined the USAAF and flew five combat missions as an air gunner in the 351st BG, exchanging, or so it was said, the second highest salary in America — $357,000 — for his army pay of $600. During his time in the 8th Air Force, he made an air gunnery training film and toured a number of bases, including this one in Norfolk. Such was Gable's appeal, it was said that Goering had offered the equivalent of £5,000, plus promotion and leave, to the airmen who shot him down.

Col Frank Robinson, the CO of the Shipdham-based 44th BG, was the envy of all his men when he found himself arm-in-arm with film stars Kay Francis and Martha Raye, during their visit to the base on December 9, 1942. The sophisticated Francis, star of a succession of movies throughout the 1930s, and comedienne Raye, who had just featured in the hit screwball comedy *Hellzapoppin,* were to star together two years later in the semi-documentary *Four Girls In A Jeep,* a tale of glamour girls entertaining the troops.

Former café singer turned movie actress Irene Manning (real name, Inez Harvuot) struck a glamorous pose when she took a photo call at Snetterton, home of the 96th BG, on November 17, 1944. In that same year Manning, who had earlier starred alongside James Cagney in the classic *Yankee Doodle Dandy*, featured in the musicals *The Desert Song* and *Shine On, Harvest Moon*.

The dapper French-American Adolphe Menjou had the reputation of being Hollywood's best-dressed man, but he proved he also had a comic touch during his appearance on stage at Hethel on August 30, 1943.

Eddie Rickenbacker, seen here meeting one of the Red Cross girls at Shipdham, was an inspirational figure to the crews of the USAAF. As a fighter pilot during World War One, the one-time motor-racing driver chalked up 26 victories, making him America's 'ace of aces'. It was a record subsequently recognised by the award of a Medal of Honor and it became a target for a new generation of aces, of the calibre of Bodney-based Mustang pilot George Preddy, to beat.

Aside from film stars, the biggest crowd-pullers were sporting heroes. Cpl Billy Conn, the former world light heavyweight boxing champion (1939-40), visited a number of bases around Norfolk. Conn, who had gone 13 rounds with Joe Louis before being ko'd in his bid to take the heavyweight title in 1941, is seen here at Hethel, inside the ring in an exhibition bout and surrounded by his fans. Interestingly, Louis also did a tour of bases in Norfolk. The pair did not meet again in the ring, however, until 1946 when Louis triumphed by an eighth-round knockout.

The visit of British Foreign Minister, Anthony Eden, to Shipdham in June 1943, was a more formal affair designed to cement relations between the Allies. Alongside him were Captain Robert E.Miller's crew, lined up either side of their aircraft *Rum Runner,* and, far right, General Jacob Devers.

Plain Jimmy Stewart

THE man they called the 'tall drawl' ran a finger over the crumpled runway map, searching for the landmarks of distant memories.

"The only thing I can really orientate on is the control tower", he confessed. "The living quarters were away from the runway, and I remember they seemed to be very low, sorta sunk into the ground."

He had been back years earlier, long before the tower had started its descent into ruin. "I remember," he added, "during the war we used to go into Norwich and sometimes into the village, but I can't remember much of it now. We always seemed to be busy then, you know..."

The instantly recognisable voice belonged to Hollywood film actor James Stewart. The memories, however, belonged to plain Jimmy Stewart, B-24 pilot and one-time commander of the 703rd Squadron, 445th Bombardment Group based at Tibenham. Stewart had turned his back on an MGM contract, reckoned to be worth more than £40,000 a year, to enlist as a private in the army eight months before America entered the war.

Studio bosses were stunned at his decision. Stewart was 32-years-old, and at the pinnacle of his success. Only days before becoming Private 0-433 210 with a monthly wage of $21, he had been the toast of Hollywood, scooping the Best Actor Oscar for his part in *The Philadelphia Story.*

Stewart, however, was deadly serious about his sudden change of career and, unlike so many of his fellow stars in uniform, he was determined to see action at the sharp end.

He achieved his ambition at Tibenham, Station 124, where he arrived in 1943, following spells as a flying instructor, training film narrator and squadron operations officer. Any airmen who thought his appointment was merely an exercise in public relations were quickly disabused. Captain Jimmy Stewart was not out for an easy ride.

In fact, as CO of the 703rd Squadron, he clocked up 20 combat missions, earning a reput-ation among his crews as something of a lucky talisman. For his own part, Stewart, like so many other commanders, was worn by the strain of the unremitting bombing offensive. He later recorded: "I was really afraid of what the dawn might bring. Our group had suffered several casualties during the day and the next morning at dawn I was going to have to lead my squadron out again, deep into Germany. I got to imagining what might happen and I feared the worst. Fear is an insidious and deadly thing; it can warp judgement, freeze reflexes, breed mistakes. And worse, it's contagious. I could feel my own fear and I knew that if it wasn't checked it could infect my crew members."

He decided to visit the base chapel.

"I guess it was because I kept being reminded that life can be short that I turned to religion. If you think you might die at any moment you think more about the hereafter. Sometimes during a scary moment in the skies, I would remember the *91st Psalm* my father had taught me. I went to Chapel regularly. It was a bad period. Many men I flew with were being killed in action. Religion meant a lot to me for the rest of the war."

That Stewart succeeded in conquering his fears was reflected in the award of the Distinguished Flying Cross for his courageous leadership during a raid on Brunswick. Once, while leading an attack on Ludwigshaven, a shell burst just beneath his wing, but he managed to keep control and bombed the target. On another occasion, to the consternation of his crew, he had flown an unarmed, multi-coloured assembly ship with a force of B-24s against Bordeaux.

By the end of the war, he wore the ribbons of the DFC, the Air Medal and one oak-leaf cluster and the French Croix de Guerre with Palm.

The future film actor Walter Matthau, then an NCO serving in Norfolk, later recorded: "I used to go to briefings just to listen to him, just to hear him do his Jimmy Stewart. I watched the way the new crews would relate to him. They

Stars at war. Jimmy Stewart took part in 20 combat missions as a pilot of a B-24, while Clark Gable clocked up five missions as an air gunner before rotating back to the States.

Jimmy Stewart in classic pose, on the control tower at either Tibenham or Old Buckenham.

Damage to *Nine Yanks And A Jerk*, one of the B-24s Jimmy Stewart flew while serving at Tibenham with the 445th BG.

used to relate to him as though he were a movie star for a while, then they'd forget about all that and realise he was one of the boys. He was marvellous to watch."

Stewart's wartime career took him from Tibenham to Old Buckenham, where he served as Operations Officer of the 453rd bombardment Group from March until July 1944, and on to Ketteringham Hall, as Lieut Col Stewart, Chief of Staff of the 2nd Combat Wing, 8th USAAF. In the process, he had clocked up more than 1,800 hours. Of his 20 missions, 14 had been flown as wing leads and one as the division leader. The gawky, stammering screen star who appeared to epitomise the virtues of small-town America had indeed travelled a long way from Tinsel Town.

A rare shot of Stewart taken after he had flown into Hardwick in early 1944.

As operations officer of the 453rd BG at Old Buckenham, it was Stewart's job to debrief returning crews. He is seen here with (left to right) 2nd Lieut Robert F.Sullivan, Capt Ray L.Sears, pilot of the *Spirit of Notre Dame* and 1st Lieut

Arthur Cromarty following a raid on Berlin.

Four days before the end of the war in Europe, Lieut Col Stewart was decorated with the Croix de Guerre with Palm by Marechal Valin, Chief of Staff for the French Air Force, during a colourful ceremony at Ketteringham Hall. Stewart was one of a number of 8th Air Force officers and men honoured for 'exceptional services' in the liberation of France.

Stewart, in leather jacket, on the control tower at Old Buckenham.

Stewart returned to Tibenham on September 14, 1975, to open the Norfolk Gliding Club air show. Thick cloud and rain grounded most of the planned displays, but Stewart delighted visitors by touring his old strip in an open-top Land-Rover with *'Old Glory'* fluttering proudly behind.

In June 1975, during a private visit, Jimmy Stewart took to the air above Tibenham once again, only this time he was strapped into a twin-controls glider as guest of the Norfolk Gliding Club. His flight took him over Old Buckenham and later in the day he flew to RAF Coltishall, where he made a lightning inspection of the Memorial Flight before being saluted by a fly-past from a single Spitfire.

A few days later, making an emotional visit to the 2nd Air Division Memorial Library in Norwich, later to be destroyed by fire.

Back to Old Buckenham. Plain Jimmy Stewart takes a lone walk across the remains of the runway at his wartime base on May 30, 1983, when he joined fellow veterans of the 453rd BG and their relatives on a pilgrimage which saw him plant an American tulip tree in the grounds of the village hall as a symbol of the friendship which has endured for more than 50 years.

Memorable Flights

Cripes 'A Mighty 3rd
August 9, 1944

BODNEY had witnessed some grand binges in its time as a fighter base, but none would be more remembered than the drinking session which spilled over into the early hours of Sunday, August 6, 1944.

It was a wild night that would go down in history as the party before Major George E.Preddy became the first USAAF pilot to shoot down six German fighters in a single sortie.

A pre-war barnstormer pilot, Preddy had flown a tour in the south-west Pacific before being posted to the 352nd Fighter Group which was destined for the European theatre. Flying first the P-47 Thunderbolt and then, most notably, the P-51 Mustang, the small, skinny aviator from Greensboro, North Carolina, endured a frustrating start before reeling off a string of successes.

Between December 1, 1943 and August 15, 1944, Preddy, nicknamed 'Mouse' on account of his size, recorded at least 15 confirmed aerial victories and a number of probables.

A southerner among many northern officers, he was renowned for his courtesy and popularity with all ranks. Joe 'Red' McVay, who served as his assistant crew chief, reckons he never heard him swear. His only known exclamation was 'Cripes A'Mighty', most commonly heard in the midst of crap games, and it would be forever enshrined in USAAF folklore as the nickname given to all Preddy's aircraft.

McVay remembers: "Although the Major was only a couple of years older than I, at my age of 73 I have yet to find a man I respected more. He was a quiet man, no air of bravado about him."

They had teamed up for the first time in January 1944. At the time, Preddy, a captain with two victories to his name, was flying a P-47.

"The first day I was left alone with the plane,"

recalls McVay, "Captain Preddy was downed by flak, and wound up in the English Channel. Although he did achieve his third victory on that mission, I was afraid he might think me a jinx.

"I served with him until he shot down six planes in one mission ...By then his latest plane, *Cripes A'Mighty 3rd*, showed 31 victories on the side, and I knew he no longer thought me a jinx."

In fact, McVay detected no discernible difference throughout that period. "He was the same man many victories later as when I met him with two victories. I loved him, but more than that, all the men of the 487th Squadron loved him."

By the first week in August, Preddy was well into his fifth extension of a combat tour in which he had set his sights on overhauling the 26 victories of America's World War One ace of aces, Eddie Rickenbacker.

On August 5, he added one victory and another probable to his tally, and, with predicted foul weather expected to ground all operations the next day, Preddy celebrated with some gusto, winning $1,200 in a crap game.

But no sooner had the young ace slumped into bed, the worse for drink, than he was roused with the stunning news that there would, after all, be a mission, and furthermore it was Preddy's turn to lead it.

Despite an offer from his CO Lieut Colonel John C.Meyer, himself a high-scoring ace, to take over the mission, Preddy insisted on heading the sortie as escorts for a raid on Berlin. He scarcely looked in a fit state to fly let alone lead. During the briefing which he conducted, he stumbled and fell off the platform. But, having been given an intake of pure oxygen in an attempt to sharpen his dulled senses, he took off for what would be a six-hour mission of memorable proportions. What happened in the clear skies over Germany is best told in the words of Preddy's own combat report, filed immediately after his return to Bodney:

"I was Group Leader. We were escorting the

Major George E.Preddy poses back at Bodney for press cameramen after his outstanding combat feat.

lead combat wings of B-17s when 30-plus Me-109s in formation came into the third box from the south. We were a thousand feet above them so I led White Flight — consisting of Lieut Heyer, Lieut Doleac and myself — in astern of them. I opened fire on one near and rear of the formation from 300 yards dead astern and got many hits around the canopy.

"The E/A *(enemy aircraft)* went down inverted and in flames. At this time, Lieut Doleac became lost while shooting down a 109 that had gotten on Lieut Heyer's tail. Lieut Heyer and I continued our attack and I drove up behind another enemy aircraft getting hits around the wing roots and setting him on fire after a short burst. He went spinning down and the pilot bailed out at 20,000 feet.

"I then saw Lieut Heyer on my right shooting down another enemy aircraft. The enemy formation stayed together. Taking practically no evasive action, and tried to get back for an attack on the bombers who were off to the right. We continued with our attack on the rear end and I fired on another at close range. He went down, smoking badly, and I saw him begin to fall apart below us. At this time four other P-51s came in to help us with the attack. I fired at another 109, causing him to burn after a short burst. He spiralled down to the right in flames.

"The formation headed down in a left turn keeping themselves together in a rather close formation. I got a good burst into another one causing him to burn and spin down. The enemy aircraft were down to 5,000 feet now and one pulled off to the left. I was all alone with them now so went after this single 109 before he could get on my tail. I got in an ineffective burst causing him to smoke a little. I pulled up into a steep climb to the left above him and he climbed after me. I pulled it in tight as possible and climbed at about 150 mph. The Hun opened fire on me but could not get enough deflection to do any damage. With my initial speed I slightly outclimbed him. He fell off to the left and I dropped down astern of him. He jettisoned his canopy as I fired a short burst getting many hits. As I pulled past, the pilot bailed out at 7,000 feet.

"I had lost all contact with friendly and enemy aircraft so headed home alone.

"Claim: six (6) Me-109s."

After returning to Bodney, a rueful Preddy promised never to fly with a hangover again. According to one account, he admitted to being sick in his cockpit shortly before his fateful combat.

Preddy was recommended for the Congressional Medal of Honor for his unparalleled feat, but it was downgraded by higher authority to a Distinguished Service Cross.

Sent home for a long overdue leave, Preddy did not return to action until late October when he was promoted to command the 328th Squadron based at Bodney.

However, Preddy had added only four more successes to his score before he fell, on Christmas Day 1944, a victim of 'friendly fire' while chasing an enemy fighter at tree-top height over an American anti-aircraft battery.

It was a tragic end to a brilliant career. At the time of his death, George Preddy was the top-scoring American operating in the European theatre with 27½ aerial victories, making him the leading Mustang ace of the war.

Shortly before his final mission, the ace they called the 'Mouse' had told a journalist: "I sure as hell am not a killer, but combat flying is like a game and a guy likes to come out on top."

His death stunned the men at his home base who had come to see him as almost indestructible. 'Red' McVay remembers: "That Christmas Day, when I heard of the loss of the Major. I could not, would not, believe it. It was not true. It could not be true. It was too painful to comprehend. It still is."

And even now, half a century later, the impact of his loss continues to be felt.

"I feel great joy every year as my wife and I celebrate Christmas with our children and grandchildren," says McVay, "but I always set aside part of that day to remember George Preddy, whose life was cut short, much too short, by that tragic accident."

America's top-scoring Mustang ace of the war, George E.Preddy makes friends with a youngster at a Christmas party in 1943.

Tragedies of War

OF ALL the myriad incidents associated with the Americans in Norfolk during the war, few, if any, made a deeper impact than the aircraft crashes which scarred the landscape. No one who ever witnessed the sights of a once mighty aircraft reduced to twisted scrap, scorched black by fire and with personal papers and equipment scattered all around, could ever forget it.

They brought home like nothing else the full horror of the unrelenting air offensive waged against Hitler's Reich. A war in which the civilian population could sometimes feel divorced from the grim reality was suddenly made shockingly real as the hazards being undertaken and the sacrifices being made were revealed.

In a region criss-crossed with airfields, it was inevitable perhaps that such sights should become an all-too familiar feature of the conflict.

The causes of the crashes were many and varied. Mechanical problems, fuel shortages and mid-air collisions took their tragic toll. But the majority of aircraft that came down were victims of battle damage as they sought desperately to make the last leg of their return from missions over enemy-occupied Europe.

Frequently, they came back with engines shot out. Often, they had injured men on board in need of urgent medical treatment. For men such as these the saying 'on a wing and a prayer' was all too real.

Al Winant, a radio operator who served with the 452nd BG at Deopham Green, remembers just such an occasion, following a raid on Bordeaux on June 19, 1944.

His B-17, *Ain't Misbehavin' II*, had suffered flak strikes over the target which holed the wings and jammed the bomb doors shut.

He recalls: "We were separated from our group — visibility was very poor. We headed back towards England. Lost our first engine from punctured gas tanks. Losing altitude we lost our second engine over the Channel. Still losing altitude and flying on two engines now, we thought of ditching ...I sent an SOS signal and

Smoke billows from *Ain't Misbehavin' II* in a field near Wattisham shortly before her cargo of 20 250lb bombs exploded.

This shot of a 452nd BG Fortress at Deopham Green offers graphic illustration of the punishment some B-17s withstood.

Crews even faced risks on their own bases. This 96th BG B-17 had a narrow escape when it collided with a petrol bowser at Snetterton without exploding.

was picked up at Harwich, so we knew they were tracking us. But we made the English coast. Our pilot ...had an airfield ahead. Just then, we lost our third engine. I remember seeing our left wing tip hitting a tree top and we hit the ground. There was lots of dust and smoke. Our last engine, I believe No.2, caught fire ...I got out through a hole in the waist, where the fuselage cracked open, also the tail and waist gunners.

"We pulled our pilot, co-pilot, navigator, engineer and bombardier out through the nose hatches. I remember yelling at the people coming through the field to help. We were yelling to get away. There were bombs still aboard. We were running towards a nearby hedgerow when the bombs exploded. The concussion waves knocked us all down and we were hit by pieces. We were taken to the base hospital where the medics patched up our cuts ...We went back to see what was left of our plane. On the way we saw some of the damage on the base ...part of a wing spar and a piece of propeller sticking in the tennis court. When we got to where our plane was — nothing but a large V-shaped hole ...I looked at that hole where *Ain't Misbehavin' II* was two hours ago and knew that God was with us on that crash."

For the children, who lived within sight and sound of the huge air bases, too young to comprehend the true nature of the conflict, such dramas served merely to heighten their excitement.

To them crashed aircraft usually meant only one thing, a source of souvenirs. Everything, from shellcases, pieces of perspex to fragments of shrapnel, were highly prized. Dick Wickham, then a teenager at Harleston, on the Norfolk-Suffolk border, recalls one memorable expedition which began while cycling back to school around lunchtime on January 30, 1943.

Together with a friend, he spotted a Flying Fortress clearly in trouble as it circled before disappearing behind some trees. Thoughts of school vanished as they pedalled off in search of the crash site. They found it in a field near Starston, the aircraft lying on its belly.

The identification letter 'D' on the tailplane told them that the aircraft belonged to 100 BG based at Thorpe Abbotts. The aircraft, *Sunny II*, had been returning from its 14th mission when it came down.

The crew were standing by the road, and a guard had been posted on the aircraft.

"We waited until the truck had left with the crew and tentatively asked the guard if we might have a closer look at the Fort. To our amazement he replied, 'Sure, but don't touch anything.' The Fortress had skidded into the middle of a field. I think it had broken its back at the point of the ball turret. I remember everything inside the fuselage was still warm and things were still ticking and creaking. Being teenage boys we saw no danger from the aeroplane and were soon inside it. There was a strong smell of petrol and oil fumes ...This was the first time I had been inside a Fortress ...Every bit of the aircraft was explored, from the nose to the tail. One thing I noticed was that the bombardier had removed the bomb sight.

"We both climbed into the cockpit and flew another mission in it. We were brought back into reality by an American officer banging on the side of the fuselage and telling us to get out."

They returned to the aircraft over the next few days to watch it being gradually devoured by a salvage squad. The perspex nose had miraculously survived the crash only to be smashed to smithereens while being hoisted on to a lorry.

"We gathered as many pieces as we could to keep as souvenirs. When the officer in charge saw how keen we were to collect these pieces he gave us both the perspex covers of the landing lights from the leading edge of the wings, telling us to keep them under our coats. I remember this cover fitted perfectly around my body under my coat, that's how I got it home out of view ...I cannot remember what happened to it once I got it home. If only I had it now..."

The enthusiasm of youth was entirely understandable. But there were times when brutal reality contrived to invade the world of

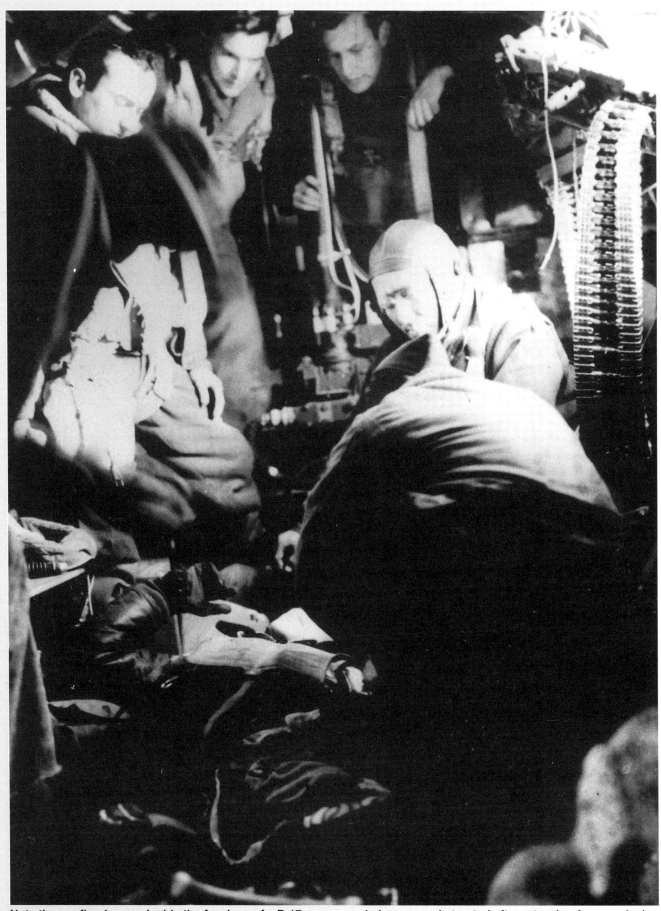

Note the confined space inside the fuselage of a B-17 as a wounded crewman is treated after returning from a mission to Deopham Green.

A ghostly mist veils the wreckage of B-24 *52359* in the depths of Langley Woods where she crashed after a mid-air collision.

schoolboy innocence. As an air cadet, aged 14½, Ron Park spent a week at RAF Oulton during the summer of 1943. He saw a number of damaged American bombers make forced landings at the base and recalls how one had sustained such severe damage 'that its return was nothing short of a miracle':

"The aeroplane had been attacked by fighters and had been hit by anti-aircraft fire. There were several large holes in the fuselage, one of them almost big enough for a man to walk through, and more holes in the wings. One side of the tailplane had been blown off and there was a large piece of the tail fin and rudder missing. The rest of the fin and the rudder was stripped of its cladding, leaving just the bare ribs. Luckily, the landing gear had been in working order and the aircraft had been able to make a normal landing but an anti-aircraft shell had burst on or close to the ball gun turret whilst the gunner had been

inside and I think that what was left of the poor chap was still inside the turret judging by the state of the interior ...I had seen a few gruesome sights during the Blitz but this was something else and I have to admit that I didn't feel like eating for the rest of the day..."

Battle casualties were bad enough, but losing crews, particularly experienced men who had survived the maelstrom of combat, to accidents was even harder to bear. Such was the awful fate which befell 1st Lieut Albert S.Broadfoot Jr and T/Sgt Selwyn Kaplan, two members of the 448th BG based at Seething, on March 13, 1945. Both Broadfoot, a 'tall, handsome full-blooded Indian', and Kaplan, a radio operator regarded as a studious type who had ambitions of becoming a diplomat, had just completed their operational tours.

But while waiting for their shipping orders back home, they and another NCO were

Airman poet Selwyn Kaplan, who died during a training flight from Seething, is third from the left on the back row of this crew snapshot.

assigned to fly a training sortie with a group of officers from a rookie crew led by pilot 2nd Lieut Paul E. Westrick. Part of the exercise involved a P-47 Thunderbolt fighter making mock attacks to give the gunners 'real life practice'.

All went off without a hitch until around 4pm. Vince Haley, who had flown with Kaplan during his 35-mission tour, recalls: "As they were coming back the pilot of the crew asked control if they could circle again in order to learn to identify the 448th field (Seething). When they did this manoeuvre, the P-47 fighter plane was buzzing them and it hit the B-24. Both aircraft crashed at Langley and all the practice crew were killed along with Selwyn."

In all, eight men died in the tragedy, including the pilot of the P-47, an aircraft which had lived up

Rookie pilot Paul E. Westrick lies buried in the Cambridge American Military Cemetery.

The twisted remains of the *Belle of Boston* disfigure the rural landscape on the fringe of Frettenham. The B-24H plunged to earth on May 8, 1944, shortly after taking off from Horsham St Faith bound for Brunswick. Of her crew of ten, six were killed and four injured. Fortunately, none of its deadly cargo of 12 500lb bombs exploded and all were safely removed.

to its unfortunate name of *Galloping Catastrophe*.

Later, while clearing out Kaplan's personal possessions, two poems which he had written were found. One of them was undated, but had almost certainly been penned after finishing a tour fraught with danger. It read:

I came to this land in search of death,
But death like life has passed me by,
Permitting me only to feel its breath,
Not having the grace to let me die.

Death like life, has played with me,
Giving and taking as in a game,
Refusing to grasp full victory,
Not knowing it seems, the sport grows tame.

Returning from a raid on Merseburg/Leuna on July 29, 1944, B-17 *Gin Rickey* from 338th BS, 96th BG, was forced to put down in a field short of the Snetterton runway. Three men died in the crash, one man was injured and five got clear of the wreckage unharmed.

Running short of fuel, Liberator *Broad and High*, from 788 BS, 467th BG based at Rackheath, ploughed a trail through a farmer's field of sugar beet at Kirby Bedon at 6.55pm, on August 18, 1944 after suffering flak damage during a mission to Woippy. Tragically, the aircraft hit a ridge and crushed the nose section, resulting in the deaths of four crew members. By a quirk of fate, the pilot, Lieut Roger L.Leister, was the only one from the five remaining crewmen to escape injury. The four men who died are recorded on a memorial plaque in Kirby Bedon Church.

People living on the Larkman housing estate, in the west of Norwich, had a lucky escape in the summer of 1944 when a B-24 flying out of Horsham St Faith was forced to make a perilous crash landing opposite the Oval pub in Costessey. The bomber, piloted by Captain Fred O'Neill, was flying at 900ft above the city on a test flight when all four engines suddenly cut out. Fred Carr was only 16 when he saw the aircraft gliding towards a line of houses in Beecheno Road at barely rooftop height. "It didn't seem possible he could reach the fields," he recalls. "The last house in the way was my father's, but incredibly the pilot managed it, just missing our chimney before pancaking in a cloud of dust." Captain O'Neill walked away from the wreck unharmed to later pose beside the crashed bomber and to be feted by grateful residents who presented him with a commemorative clock.

Boyds Boids was only seconds away from home after a harrowing return flight from Germany when disaster threatened to overtake the Snetterton-based B-17 on November 21, 1944. Limping home on two engines at little more than wave-top height, the 96th BG Fortress was lining up to land when another B-17 with wounded crewmen aboard cut in ahead of them. Too low and with insufficient power to make a second attempt, *Boyds Boids* came down yards from the airfield perimeter, straddling and totally blocking the LNER Norwich-London railway line near Bryant's Bridge. Fortunately, there was no fire and although all of the crew were injured, some of them seriously, none were killed.

This Liberator's mission on New Year's Eve 1944 ended unceremoniously on open land near Hall Farm, Beetley. Returning from a mission, B-24 *J 44-10528* ran out of fuel as it made its final run-in towards its home base at Wendling. It was the last 2nd Division B-24 to be written-off in a crash in Norfolk and Suffolk in 1944. Dennis Duffield, a youngster at the time, recalled: "It was a Sunday afternoon, about 2.45pm, and my father and I were out poaching rabbits. Suddenly, we saw a lot of flares and we ran back. When we reached the field, the aircraft laid there and all the crew just stood around. They'd feathered all four engines before hitting the ground. I spoke to them and they gave us their candy. But we lost our dinner because of all that." The plane laid in the field until March, by which time a salvage team had removed the aircraft's machine guns and Dennis recovered the control column and instrument panel as souvenirs of the day a Liberator fell to earth and interrupted his poaching expedition.

A pall of thick black smoke rises above Snetterton airfield as flames ravage Lieut Len Kramer's 96th BG B-17 *43-38576*. Landing too close to another Fortress from the same squadron on December 28, 1944, Kramer collided and his aircraft caught fire. Fortunately, all of his crew got clear, but the plane was a write-off. Despite severe damage, the other B-17 flew again and no one aboard her was injured.

The tangled scraps of wreckage scattered across the snow-carpeted fields of the Lophams on January 29, 1945, are reminders of one of the worst accidental tragedies of the war waged from Norfolk's airfields. At 9.05 am, amid the drone of bombers assembling above, villagers heard the dull thud of an explosion and then watched in horror as the wintry sky rained wreckage and bodies. All 18 crew members of the two Sneterton-based 96th BG B-17s piloted by Lieut

Alex Philipovitch and Lieut George Peretti died as a result of the mid-air collision.

An airman, flying in another crew, noted in his diary: "...saw 2 ships collide when forming this morning. Philipovitch was flying one of the ships. Blew up and no one escaped. Was awful sight to see pieces of the ships go down with empty chutes in the explosion..."

The shattered remains of a rear gunner was found in the tail-section of Philipovitch's aircraft which drifted down near Gables Farm. One airman was not recovered for several days. Part of one aircraft's bombload fell into the main street at North Lopham, but fortunately none had been armed and danger was minimal. Miraculously, no one on the ground was injured. It later emerged that Lieut Peretti's ill-starred B-17 had been involved in another fatal collision three months earlier when a P-47 pilot was killed after his plane struck the bomber's tail while making a simulated attack during a training exercise.

The hazards of flying out of a base on the edge of a large residential area were exposed once more on February 13, 1945, when B-24 *A Dog's Life,* from the 458th BG at Horsham St Faith, crashed at Old Catton. Two engines cut out during a practice flight and the aircraft, piloted by Lawrence W.Shannon, was seen to go into a spin from about 800ft before plunging into a house at the junction of Spixworth Road and Church Street. All nine crew members died in the conflagration which followed and one woman civilian was injured.

The end of the war was barely three weeks away when Seething became the setting for a tragedy which would live forever in the memory of all those who witnessed it. These jagged pieces of metal near the end of Runway 25 are all that remained of B-24 *M 44-50572* after the aircraft crashed and blew up shortly after taking off for a mission against Lanshut on April 16, 1945.

This tragic flight was to have been the crew's 13th mission. Tail gunner Ed Paretti (third left of the front row of the crew photograph) recalled: "After being tossed around a little, the aircraft came to a stop and there was fire and ammunition exploding somewhere on board ...I believe the aircraft was resting on the tail skid which left just enough room to squeeze out. Because of the bombload and full load of fuel, my first intent was to get away from the aircraft."

In all six crewmen scrambled out of the bomber, but four were trapped between the pilots' seats and the top turret which had broken off.

"Suddenly," added Paretti, "a huge fire broke out around Nos. 3 and 4 engines and everyone ran for cover."

William Schwinn was one of many men who rushed from all corners of the base to try and help the men trapped. But although the aircraft was quickly surrounded by would-be rescuers they lacked the equipment needed to cut through the wreckage.

"You could hear them hollering and pounding on the thing to 'get them out'", remembered Schwinn, "and ...out of the clear blue someone yelled loud as they could to 'leave it' ...We started running away and we hadn't gotten too far away when this thing exploded. It felt like a big hand that reaches out and pushes you in the back and you had a problem to stay upright because the concussion was so great."

Further away men on the base saw a ball of flame rise above a line of trees followed by a mushroom of thick black smoke. All four men were killed instantly, and the fact that they had died within sight and sound of so many comrades powerless to help served only to make the sense of shock all the more profound.

Schwinn recorded: "Those are the sort of things that stay with you. They stay with you for a long time..."

Local firefighters could do little but stand and watch when a C-109 Liberator Tanker laden with 6,000 gallons of petrol bound for the Continent crashed among buildings at Harling Farm, East Harling, at 1.05pm, on January 8, 1945. The five-man crew all died in the inferno. Today, they are remembered on a cement memorial at the site of the crash.

Unhappy landing. A salvage team clamber over a B-24 at Seething which has come to grief in a sea of mud.

Another base, another salvage team. This time it's Shipdham, where the party are examining the wreck of Lieut William M.Duffy's 506th Squadron B-24 which swerved off the west end of the main runway while taking off for a raid on Merignac in France on March 5, 1944. It was the 44th BG's 190th mission. Note the four-legged friend taking an interest in the smashed nose!

Local people came to the rescue of a crewman trapped in the wreckage of B-24 *41-29168F* which crashed-landed on Frogshall Farm, near Southrepps on November 13, 1943, after sustaining battle damage during a raid on Bremen. William Riseborough and J.Fox struggled for hours through rain and fading light before successfully freeing the navigator, 1st Lieut F.L.Jope. Later, they received a letter of commendation from Brigadier General Walter R.Peck in which he wrote: "Your initiative and untiring labors in tunnelling under the crashed aircraft and cutting away a portion of the fuselage undoubtedly resulted in saving the life of this seriously injured airman."

Next page, top: A gigantic fireball trails a pillar of smoke as it mushrooms above a line of Liberators. In this fatal moment a blazing bomber is blown to smithereens. Seven more aircraft are damaged. The blast rocked a row of houses bordering the airfield at Horsham St Faith and rattled windows across Norwich. The date was March 14, 1945 and the devastating explosion took place as a group of B-24s from the 458th BG were preparing to raid railway marshalling yards at Holxwickede in Germany — their 203rd sortie of the war. The bombed-up Liberator from the 753rd Squadron had fallen victim to a freak accident.

Former armaments sergeant Elliot Bim Bruner recalled: "One of the ball turret gunners was checking out his gun, which he wasn't supposed to do, and as he turned round, the gun fired and hit the plane next to it, immediately setting it on fire."

As the flames spread towards the bomb bay desperate efforts were made to move the aircraft closest to the burning B-24. The first bombs exploded at 9.38am. Civilian ambulances were called to the base as fears grew that the fire could spread to a nearby bomb dump. It was nearly two hours later before the fire was reported under control. But it had been a close-run thing. Incredibly, there had been no fatalities and the mission went ahead as planned!

Next page, bottom: The terrible moment when tragedy befell a bomber crew within 100 yards of their home base at Old Buckenham on February 9, 1945. B-24 *J 42-50703*, a lead ship with the 734th BS, 453rd BG, was returning from a raid on Magdeburg. It was the 27th mission for pilot 1st Lieut Robert G.Rollins and his crew. The wheels had been lowered for landing when a fatal misjudgement by one of the returning Liberators resulted in a collision which saw Rollins' port tail-plane sliced off. The aircraft crashed at Bury's Hall Farm killing all 11 men on board.

Letters Home

IT WAS the summer of 1944 when 2nd Lieut Rodney B.Ives, a navigator, and his crew were posted to join the 453rd BG at Old Buckenham. Since the opening of the Second Front in Normandy in June, the war had taken on a fresh intensity. By August, when Ives' crew started their tour, final victory was in their sights, but there was much hard fighting to be done before it was achieved. In a series of letters to his parents, Ives charted his progress from fledgling bomber crewman to combat-hardened veteran. They provide a vivid insight into the way of life of a young airman going to war from the fields of Norfolk...

August 13, 1944
Dear Mom
Well we have finally arrived at the 'Promised Land' — our permanent station...I really like it here. The food is tops — fried chicken and trimmings with freshly sliced tomatoes today — and good quarters. We live in Nissen huts — those round topped iron jobs you've seen pictured in newspapers — but they are fixed up swell and are really comfortable...We are really getting close to the war now. Last night we saw the RAF heavies go out and it's really an impressive sight. I'm getting very eager to get my 'baptism of fire'...
Love Rod

August 24, 1944
Dear Mom
Combat conditions are really tough. I'm sitting in a comfortable officers' club with a nice cool Tom Collins in front of me after having worked myself almost to death today reading a good book while reclining upon my sack...Paris was liberated today and that's damn good news to us. It was a pretty rough target...It looks like you might have your wish come true about me getting a few missions then having this thing come to an end...I may as well see it all while I can because when this is over I'm going to be Joe College in person for about four years and you

know that I won't be doing much travelling on that $50 a month the government is going to stake me to.
Love Rod

August 23, 1944
No.1 (first mission)
Dear Mom,
Just a note to let you know that I'm a veteran now. We hit a target in Germany today.
    Although I've been trained for 2½ years...it's quite an amazing experience to realise that your fellow man is shooting at you. Of course we do more than a little death-dealing ourselves but it's all so abstract that I have no reactions to it.
    I had no fear today but I suspect that was because of my inexperience and I know I'll feel it in future raids. I wear my flak suit and helmet at all times while under enemy fire — from the examples I've seen, it pays...
Love Rod

September 8, 1944
Dear Mom and Dad
We finished our fourth today and we really became veterans on this one. It was a target in Germany again and it was our toughest to date. In the first place we had to get up where the temperature was 40 below and then we got hit over the target. We ended up with 25 holes in our ship and two men slightly wounded...everyone took it damn good today and I think everyone was scared — I know I was — but I kept working and, now after a hot shower and a drink, it's a long way off...
Love Rod

September 12, 1944
Dear Mom and Dad
...You asked what I'd like for Christmas — I'd forgotten that I had to request things. There's nothing I need that I can think but I would like to have a good fruit cake and some cookies — preferably oatmeal and overnight cookies...We

Rodney Ives and his crew on August 29, 1944. Ives is standing far right on the back row. His pilot, Ray H.Conard is standing far left. In a letter to his parents dated September 3, Ives wrote: "Enclosed a picture of our crew after returning from a good long mission. This isn't our ship but we were flying it that day…"

are 'stood down' today but our crew has to go up and do a little practicing so I'll close now.
Love Rod

September 18, 1944
Dear Mom and Dad
I've had a lot of unusual experiences since my last letter — both good and bad. I guess I'd better start with our latest mission (No.7) which falls in the latter category. We hit another target in Germany and for the first time I saw our own ships shot down. Two ships in our own squadron went down and that's a hell of a sight to see a B-24 spiralling to earth as helplessly as a leaf…We took over and brought the squadron home safely getting only six holes in our own ship…We have named our ship *Heaven Can Wait* — my idea — how do you like it?

September 25, 1944
Dear Mom and Dad
Today I completed another lap of my tour with mission no. eight. It was a bit uninteresting compared to some we've had but that's all right because no one got hurt and it was easy on the nerves…

We've been to London again on another two day pass and this time I spent all of the time on having a good time and none on shopping. We got extravagant and entered an apartment between the four of us. It was really nice and we had some fine parties. I met a gal who is a private secretary…and we had a great time. She's the nicest girl I've met in England…
Rod

October 6, 1944
Dear Mom and Dad
…I received my ballot today and voted for the

The wreckage of Rodney Ives' ill-starred Liberator lies strewn across the field at Grove Farm, Park Common, Kenninghall, not far from the houses it so narrowly avoided.

first time in my life. I believe it is an honor and I exercised my right to vote against the capitalists and get the New Deal going again...
Rod

October 22, 1944
Dear Mom and Dad
We've had a mission and another pass since my last letter, in fact that is just about the regular routine since we've become a lead crew. We get one mission and then a pass — we've had more passes than money lately so on our last we decided to go to Great Yarmouth, a small town on the coast that — in peacetime — was a great resort town for vacationers. I had a swell time and it's much more economical because it's smaller than London. We were all treated royally because we were the only American officers in town...

About writing to my girlfriend over here Mom — it's a little impractical because I've changed already — the latest lives in Great Yarmouth. I guess I'm a little fickle but I don't like entanglements of any sort...

November 20, 1944
Dear Mom and Dad
I guess by now you can always tell when I'm

having a good time by the lack of letters. It is very true in this case too because at the present time I'm on leave of seven days and I also had a two day pass since my last letter...I don't think you're quite up to date on our missions. We have now completed 14...On our 13th, which we number 12a for superstition's sake, we lead (*sic*) the Wing. That means we had 90 airplanes behind us — quite a responsibility — but it went successfully.

You'll really get a laugh when I tell you where I'm spending my leave — on a farm. Hilz — the co-pilot — and myself are staying on this farm which is located about four blocks from the center of little town on the seashore. We both have girlfriends in town so this is an ideal way to spend a rest leave because we really do get plenty of rest and the best food in England. The people treat us wonderfully and it's the first time in the ETO that I've gotten all the milk and butter I wanted.

There isn't much night life in this little town but we bring our gals out to the farm and sit round the huge fireplace in the living room drinking tall cool drinks and it's really pleasant...I don't have much to do with the working end of the farm. I guess that's why I enjoy it so much here. This is the rest leave for

Navigator Al Neumunz, the man who joined Conard's crew as an extra navigator to extend his run of missions, is seated far right.

our crew but I really didn't need a rest. All of the boys say that I'm getting fat so I guess combat agrees with me...

I'm thinking about volunteering for some special duties over here...After our tour is completed we have the opportunity to sign up for some training which would fit us for the job of disarming and demobilizing the German Air Force... I'd be there from 2-5 months after hostilities had ceased but that wouldn't be bad and it's a wonderful opportunity for me to get some more travel and experience...
Love Rod

Rodney Ives was destined never to realise his ambitions. This letter, his last one, was post-marked November 26, 1944. That same day his crew were briefed to lead an attack on a railway viaduct, near Bielefeld, Germany. Included among the unusually large crew of 12 was Ives' fellow navigator, Ronald Neumunz, who had volunteered in order to complete his tour sooner. Shortly after the 734th Squadron Liberator laboured skywards from Old Buckenham it became clear the aircraft was in difficulty. Eyewitnesses saw the fully-loaded bomber struggle in vain to gain height. Moments later, as it flew over open country it was seen to disgorge its entire bomb load. Yet, still it refused to climb. Steadily losing altitude, the Liberator roared low over the bleak autumnal landscape. Suddenly, directly in her path, there loomed two houses, about 40ft apart. Unable to climb above or fly between them, the pilot, Captain Ray H.Conard, veered away in what eyewitnesses thought was a deliberate though suicidal attempt to avoid endangering civilian lives. Seconds later, the aircraft cartwheeled into the field in front of the houses killing all 12 crew but without harming any of the occupants. From take-off to fatal crash, the whole drama had lasted only six minutes.

Memorable Flights

Belle of the East
August 25, 1944

> *Bailed out close to Yarmouth. 3 men in waist rode 'er down. No severe injuries. Biggest thrill of my life...*

FRED Sammetinger's terse diary entry for August 25, 1944 was remarkable almost as much for its economy of words as for the astonishing escape that occurred that summer's day.

His single page note told, in outline, the story of his fifth mission, flown from Rackheath against the NordDeutsch Dornierwerke aviation factory in Lubeck, Germany. Thirty-three air-

craft had bombed from 22,500ft. Flak had been 'moderate', and Sammetinger recorded that one shell fragment had pierced the centre of the turret and struck the armour plate.

The real drama, however, did not begin until the 791st Squadron B-24 *Belle of the East* was almost home. Years after scribbling his original brief account, Fred Sammetinger, bombardier in the nine-man crew, told the full story:

"The mission was nothing special, rather uneventful. As per our operating procedure, when returning from a mission, we flew over our base, Rackheath, in formation. Squadrons 1 and 2 would peel off for landing while Squadron No.3 flew a circle from our northerly heading, to the right, which took us near Yarmouth.

"Our altitude on this circle was between 1,500 and 2,000ft...I was standing on the flight deck between pilot, Craig Harrington, and co-pilot,

A rare photograph of the *Belle of the East* during her operational career at Rackheath. The original name has been covered by an armour plate revealing the number of bomber missions flown.

Crew No.84, 791st Squadron, 467th BG, which were involved in the remarkable flight on August 25, 1944. They are (back row, left to right): 2nd Lieut John Boesen, navigator; 2nd Lieut Craig Harrington, pilot; 2nd Lieut Fred Sammetinger, bombardier; FO Gene McMahan, co-pilot; (front row, left to right): Sgt Charles Kordus, tail gunner; Sgt Verner Gray, waist gunner; Sgt Eugene Jacquemart, radio operator who missed the mission; Sgt Charles Grinnell, waist gunner; S/Sgt Norval Cunningham, engineer; and Sgt Thomas Lewis, ball turret gunner, who also missed the mission.

Gene McMahan. I saw the fuel pressure gauge on the No.3 engine drop to '0'...Harrington turned to the engineer, Val Cunningham (standing next to me) and told him to switch the fuel transfer levers to 'Tank to Engine to Crossfeed', where any engine could be fed from any tank.

"I turned and watched Val set the four levers to the new position. When I turned back I saw the fuel pressure gauge for No.4 engine drop to '0' also. This gave me a clear indication that we were in trouble, so I took my parachute and clipped it to the harness and headed for the bomb bay.

"The navigator, John Boesen, was at the radio operator's position and I told him to open the bomb bay doors which he did. I heard the pilot ring the emergency bell and saw the co-pilot get up from his seat and head for the bomb bay. At this point, I jumped from the plane...feet first.

"While coming down, I saw only two other chutes leave the plane...the engineer and I came down in a ploughed field just across the road from a 'spotting post'. Almost instantly, an officer from the post arrived and took us to the club for a bracer or two. While there, we were told that four other chutes had left the plane and that three gunners in the waist rode her down and were not seriously injured..."

The survival of the three men was little short of miraculous. According to Sammetinger, they were not certain about hearing the bell and were trying to contact the pilot when they realised the danger they were in. There was nothing they could do, as Marvin Berman, who was flying that day as a replacement for the regular radio operator, recalled: "We were too low to bail out."

From the ground, a number of people saw the *Belle's* shallow, gliding descent. Incredibly, it appeared as though it might make a perfect belly landing. But within a few feet of the ground, she struck an oak tree. Both wings were torn off and the fuselage demolished pig-stys and fruit trees before hitting a drainage ditch and flipping over on to its back on ground close to Goffins Lane, now known as Sandy Lane, Belton, a few miles south of Yarmouth.

Berman recorded: "I remember hearing glass breaking. I later was told the left wing hit a greenhouse."

Although badly shaken, all three men were alive. Berman, with a head wound, was the worst injured and, as he crawled out of the wreckage, he was comforted by a local woman who had dashed to the crash scene. He later recalled how she had knelt down beside him 'put my head in her lap and tried to wipe the blood away.'

The woman was 26-year-old Grace Claxton, from Station Road, Belton. She was one of four villagers who rushed to the rescue without thought for their own safety.

Walter Sharman found one crewman who had just scrambled out of the wreckage and, with the help of Cliff Gray, helped release a second airman. As they were doing so, Miss Claxton and her uncle, Harry Page, approached from the other side and freed the third man.

One of the rescuers, Harry Botwright later recalled: "Two were all right, but one chap was dazed. He'd got head injuries and we helped him out 'cause we didn't know what was going to happen. It was about 15 minutes before an ambulance arrived. The airman's head was bandaged and he was put on a stretcher and four of us carried him out to the road...we stood there afterwards for a little while and, hearing a hissing noise, we ran and hid behind a muck heap."

Later, an investigation revealed that there had been 300 gallons of fuel in the *Belle's* tanks. A vapour lock was blamed as the cause of the crash. The discovery of so much fuel served to highlight not merely how lucky the three men had been but the selfless courage displayed by the villagers. All four were later officially commended for their brave actions 'in the face of what might have been imminent danger'.

Bird's-Eye View

The street plan of west Norwich merges with the fields beyond as a trio of Liberators follow the 458th assembly ship, the *Spotted Ape.*

Horsham Liberators head out towards the north Norfolk coast to formate at the start of a mission. Cromer, with its tall church tower, can just be glimpsed on the far left of the photograph.

Griston Church tower and the huge twin T2 hangars identifies this as the site of the 3rd Strategic Air Depot at Watton. Five B-24s can be seen on the ground, undergoing repairs or modifications at the Depot which served the entire 2nd Air Division.

Another church, another village. This time Hempnall, in south Norfolk, with Liberators from the 93rd Bombardment Group based at Hardwick, including the assembly ship *Ball of Fire,* making a low pass.

The shark-teethed nose of *K-Bar,* a Shipdham-based 44th BG Liberator banking over mid-Norfolk with the village of Wicklewood in the background. *K-Bar,* piloted by John I.Scarborough, was wrecked in March 1944. Limping home from a raid on Friedrichshafen with one engine out of action, *K-Bar* crashed-landed at Woodchurch, Kent. Seven men, including Scarborough, were killed and three survived.

A magnificent photograph of the veteran Snetterton-based 96th BG Fortress *Stingy* flying over the Norfolk coast on a public relations exercise. *Stingy* and a seven-man crew was lost on October 11, 1944, when she was involved in a three-plane training accident over Towcester in Northamptonshire.

The war was almost over when this flight of B-24s flew over Holkham Hall, bottom right, with the sweeping sands of the north Norfolk coast beyond. The aircraft from 506 Squadron, the last to arrive at Shipdham, home of the 44th BG, were making a practice flight on April 24, 1945.

A line of Liberators on the loop hard-stands bordering Dakenham Farm at Rackheath. On the right of the line is the *Witchcraft,* arguably the most famous Norfolk-based B-24 of all. The 467th BG aircraft clocked up a staggering total of 130 missions and was reputed never to have aborted a sortie through mechanical failure. Such was

her reliability that her ground crew, seen here replacing
an engine, were all honoured — the crew chief receiving
a Bronze Star and oak-leaf cluster.

The aircraft in the middle of a field, near the village of Ashill, was *Pregnant Peg,* the B-24 which made a piece of flying history on December 13, 1943. During assembly for a mission on October 30, the Wendling-based 578th BS, 392nd BG Liberator had experienced engine trouble. Her crew jettisoned its bombload of incendiaries near Holme Hale, fortunately without causing any casualties, and then made a forced landing in the field. Apart from a collapsed nose wheel, the aircraft escaped almost undamaged, and it was decided, instead of dismantling the bomber, to repair it in situ and attempt to fly it out.

A makeshift runway was scraped in the field and everything was done to lighten the aircraft. Eventually, in fading light, at 5.30pm on December 13, pilot Major Allen G.Russell, the Chief of Operations for the 8th Air Force Service Command's Ferry and Transport Service, released the brakes and swerved the ship on to the rough runway with a thunderous roar.

A report noted: "The wheels skidded round the turn in eight inches of mud. There was a breathless moment as the Lib rolled forward faster and faster and then its silhouette rose against the twilight sky. *Pregnant Peg* was airborne again."

It was the first time that a B-24 had been successfully flown out from a non-airfield site and the feat contributed towards a rare non-combat DFC for Russell. Sadly, *Pregnant Peg* was lost three months later when she crashed in the North Sea after being damaged by flak. Her crew of nine were all killed.

B-24s of the 44th BG in formation over Wicklewood. They are *Hitler's Nightmare* (S), *Blackjack* (X) and the legendary *Suzy Q* (L). One of the Group's original aircraft, named after Major Howard Moore's three-year-old daughter, the apparently indestructible *Suzy Q* was selected by Col Leon Johnson as his lead plane for the Ploesti raid.

Liberators of the 458th BG, from Horsham St Faith, flying over the outline of Rackheath's newly constructed but still unused airstrip in February 1944. The base was originally earmarked for a force of RAAF Lancasters, and a number of test landings had been made. But there was a change of plan, and in March 1944, the B-24s of the 467th BG arrived. Halfway up on the left of the photograph the outline of a decoy airfield for Horsham St Faith can just be seen, while on the right is the wood where two B-24s sustained mortal damage during a 'blind' take-off in thick fog on December 29, 1944.

A later photograph of Rackheath with the main runway slicing through the middle of the frame. A flare is burning in the centre of the base, the aircraft having just returned from a mission. The staff car is waiting to pick up the CO.

Patients Come First

THE colonel with a broad smile, broader chest and impressive band of medal ribbons had a simple motto for his new command in the heart of Norfolk: The patients come first. Linwood M.Gable was as good as his word, and the American Army Air Force Hospital which operated on the site of today's Wymondham College became widely-acknowledged as one of the most efficient in the country.

Gable was the ideal choice to lead the 231st Station Hospital unit on their transatlantic mission. A World War One veteran, he had served as a British Army surgeon and wore gallantry awards from both Britain and the United States. Perhaps influenced by his experiences amid the wretched squalor of the trenches, he set out not only to provide the best quality patient care, but to raise morale at the same time. The 231st moved to Morley in March 1944, some seven months after the first medical units had taken over the site. The emergency hospital, built under the lend-lease agreement, emerged on what had been the Mid-Norfolk Golf Course, in the grounds of Morley Hall.

During the next two years it would serve the needs of 15 heavy bomber bases, a fighter group, support services and, after D-Day, American troops wounded in the liberation of western Europe.

The site catered for almost every conceivable injury and illness. The mass of buildings, many of them Nissen huts, included an operating wing,

isolation ward, decontamination and dental centres and a wing for the treatment of VD as well as a chapel and rows of living quarters. In the midst of it all, however, there were reminders of the site's rural roots — a flower-fringed duck pond and a 15-acre vegetable farm cultivated by a British army corporal which helped supplement the diet of patients and staff.

The hospital staff proved popular with servicemen and locals alike. They staged children's parties and dances. Bernice Pegg, who remembers the hospital as a 'bee hive' alive with activity, recalls: "Everyone got on well together, the Americans were generous and kind."

Every Sunday afternoon an 'open house' was held at the hospital club attended by girls from the surrounding area. Pamela Standley recalls: "We were picked up by an American ambulance from Morley ...and we were chaperoned — I think that would be the right word — by a Mrs Pratt of the British Red Cross. I did go to the wards to talk to the other patients and saw that some had been terribly wounded. They seemed to be grateful to see us."

John Rex, a member of the 987th Military Police Company's Detachment 'B' stationed at the hospital, had an easy time compared with his colleagues on duty in Norwich. He remembers: "I'm one of those Yanks who fell in love with Norfolk ...from my own experience, I am proud to say that the relationship between the American servicemen and the local people was, as you would say in Norfolk, 'top of the shop!'"

Patients enjoy an outdoor concert performed by the US Army Band in what is now the school's main car park. The building in the left background was the boiler house.

The Wymondham Church Army mobile canteen, seen here in late, 1944, was a regular visitor to the 231st Station Hospital

A general view of the hospital, looking east from the sick bay entrance, with the mortuary, left, the hospital water tower, centre, and the administration block complete with telephone exchange, right.

The portly, smiling figure of Lieut Col Linwood M.Gable, commander of the hospital at Morley, and his executive officer, Lieut Col Richard B.Warriner.

Memorable Flights

Bold Venture III
December 25, 1944

IT WAS a Christmas Day Paul Ehrlich would never forget. Festive celebrations were postponed indefinitely as 30 Liberator crews at a wintry Rackheath airstrip were briefed for a raid on railway yards at Musch, in Germany.

Nine days earlier, Hitler had launched his tanks through the Ardennes forest in a desperate charge which would go down in history as the Battle of the Bulge.

As 1st Lieut Ehrlich and his crew climbed aboard the B-24 *Bold Venture III* in the early hours of December 25, 1944, the fate of many of his countrymen locked in combat in the snow-shrouded fields of Belgium hung in the balance.

Their task was to dislocate the German army's communications and prevent supplies from reaching the front-line. It proved to be Ehrlich's last and most eventful mission of the war. All went well for the 467th BG's Liberators until they began their final run-in towards the target. Flak flecked the sky as they began their bombing run. Keeping position below and behind the 788th Squadron flight leader, *Bold Venture III* was shaken by one near miss which damaged the tailplane, making rudder control difficult.

Ehrlich pressed on and successfully dropped his bomb load, but *Bold Venture III* had fallen behind the rest of the flight. He was still trying to catch up when 5 FW190s pounced. Almost immediately, one Liberator was shot out of formation, and as it fell the fighters homed in on *Bold Venture III*.

Ehrlich later wrote: "I attempted to close in on

Sheet metal repairmen pose in front of their charges at Rackheath. Behind them stands B-24J *42-50675 Bold Venture III* of the 788th Bombardment Squadron which made an amazing 300-mile flight with nobody at the controls.

The only known picture
showing the aircraft's name.
The dark panel below is a fire
extinguisher stowage point.

the leader when we received 20mm hits in the No.2 engine. We shut it down, and had just feathered the prop when I was hit in the chin and legs and was quite senseless for a short time. When I recovered, there was a fire below the flight deck on the pilot's side of the aircraft, presumably in the hydraulic system.

"I engaged the auto-pilot and hit the alarm bell to signal the crew to abandon ship. My oxygen mask was destroyed by the hit and, between the concussion and the lack of oxygen, I guess that I wasn't

Former pilot Paul Ehrlich, seen here in the 2nd Air Division Memorial Library in Norwich in 1992 after receiving a plaque containing pieces of wreckage found on the *Bold Venture III* crash site.

functioning on all cylinders. I can remember the heat from the fire on my face. I went out through the bomb bay and, as I was falling, I realised that I was passing out. I told myself to pull the ripcord because I might not get another chance. I then passed out and when I regained consciousness, I was floating down.

"The left-hand glove and my shoes came off, I presume, when the chute opened. The glove on my right remained in place because my hand was clenched, holding on to the ripcord handle. I used the glove to hold up a flap of tissue that hung down from my chin and, in so doing, was able to stop the blood flow.

"I remember a P-51 fighter circling around me all the way to the ground from approximately 20,000ft, thereby preventing any further attack from the enemy fighters."

Three other members of the crew, the co-pilot, radio operator and engineer, had followed him out. They all came down inside enemy-held territory, north of St Vith, and were soon taken prisoner.

Meanwhile, on board *Bold Venture III* a drama of a different kind was being enacted. In the confusion of the fighter attack neither the three crewmen in the nose nor the three gunners in the rear of the aircraft had heard the alarm bell sound. It was only when the navigator received no reply to his instruction for a new course heading that they decided to investigate. 1st Lieut Challenger Whitham, the pilotage navigator, and 2nd Lieut John Beyer, the bombardier, climbed up on to the flight deck and, to their astonishment, found it deserted.

Beyer recorded: "The ship was flying on C-1 auto-pilot and was making a slow circle to the left and at the time was heading back to Germany. Lieut Whitham, using the turn-control knob, began to turn the plane to a heading of 270 degrees and I went up to the nose to engage the secondary clutch on the bombsight so the auto-pilot would hold a steady heading.

"Returning to the flight deck I got into the co-pilot's seat — Lieut Whitham was in the pilot's seat …We were losing altitude at about 500ft per minute and I corrected that. Once, we encountered flak and I made some slow turns as evasive action.

In the meantime, we contacted the gunners in the waist …and told them what the situation was; that we intended to fly into France and bail out when certain that we were far from the battle lines. After flying about 30-35 minutes, the navigator said we were deep enough into friendly territory to bail out."

All six evacuated safely and landed south of Valenciennes. Their last glimpse of *Bold Venture III* was of the aircraft flying in a north-westerly direction towards what they assumed to be a watery grave somewhere in the North Sea. But they had reckoned without the Rackheath Liberator's remarkable homing instincts.

With is auto-pilot still engaged, the aircraft droned on over the Channel, making its landfall over Kent and then proceeded to traverse five counties before running out of fuel near the Welsh border, above the fogbound Herefordshire village of Vowchurch.

Farmer Ivor Davies had finished his dinner and was preparing to listen to the King's Christmas Day broadcast when he heard a strange hissing sound. Moments later, there was a knock at his door and a neighbour asked: "Where's that plane that's come down?"

The bizarre flight of *Bold Venture III* had been cut short by a tree which sent it careering across the village common, killing three cows in its path, before coming to rest in the driveway to Lower House Farm. Both wings had been torn off and the nose crushed, but the rear fuselage was almost intact. Years later, fragments of the wreckage were gathered up. Some pieces eventually found their way into the Norfolk and Suffolk Aviation Museum at Flixton. A few were fixed to a plaque and presented to Paul Ehrlich as a lasting reminder of the 2nd Air Division's aviation equivalent of the *Marie Celeste.*

GI Brides

THURSDAY, February 4, 1943, marked something of a milestone in Anglo-American relations in Norwich, remembered by thousands of Yanks as 'Liberty City'. For it was the day 18-year-old Beryl Lamb married Jim Hartzell, a USAAF bombardier from Philadelphia, and became the city's first GI bride.

The service, held at St Clement's Church, followed a whirlwind romance that had begun only in December and was hurriedly arranged before the groom left Norfolk for service in Africa. The couple did not meet again until January 1946 — in New York!

By that time, some 70,000 British girls had followed Beryl's lead by marrying Yanks 'over here'. Of these a large proportion were from East Anglia, where the concentration of air force personnel was greatest. Some were destined to end in tragedy even before the war's conclusion, others broke up, but a surprising number endured, through war and peace and the upheavals of new lifestyles 'over there', as the most tangible example of that special relationship.

One such successful GI bride was Beryl Elliott, who married PFC Horace 'Bill' Watson, a 24-year-old USAAF military policeman, at Burgh St Peter, near Yarmouth, on January 3, 1945. What follows is their story, but it stands as testament to many other happy partnerships forged in wartime...

Beryl was a girl of 13 when war broke out and living with her family in Wheatacre, near the town of Beccles. By the autumn of 1943 she was living and working in the village post office at Worlingworth. Much had happened in the intervening four years, and the pattern of the war had been irrevocably altered by the entry of the United States into the conflict. And nowhere was their presence more keenly felt than in the towns and villages that freckled the Waveney valley, where the slow-flowing river marked the border between Norfolk and Suffolk.

Beryl recalls: "When ever we went to town there were lots of Americans. They were always in the way. You saw them at dances, in the restaurants and in their jeeps, looking very busy."

While many girls of her age, attracted by the excitement and glamour which the smart, self-confident GIs appeared to offer, soon found themselves stepping out with American boyfriends, Beryl studiously ignored such dalliances:

"I did not intend for it to happen to me. I just didn't want to get involved, because I did not want to leave my home or my family."

But all of this changed one night in November 1943.

"I had a friend who was dating an American and she wanted me to go to a dance with her. I hadn't done too much of that because I was really trying to avoid the Americans. But I gave in.

"We were riding our bicycles to the dance, and 'Bill' came along in a jeep.

"He pulled alongside and asked us where we were going. I told him we were going to the village dance, and he said, 'May I come?' I replied that it was open to the public, and he said, 'Will

'Bill' and Beryl Watson on their wedding day, January 3, 1945.

The wedding of PFC William A.Vickery, a supply clerk based at Seething, and Sheila Francis at Holy Trinity Church, Loddon, on April 14, 1945 was the culmination of a 15½ month courtship. They first met on New Year's Eve 1943, three months after his arrival in Norfolk, and Vickery, who was a member of the 58th Station Complement Squadron, recalls: "Most of my time at Station 146 was spent in work and in courting Sheila." The couple who have celebrated their golden wedding anniversary make frequent return journeys to what Vickery calls his 'second home'.

Romance blossomed at Shipdham between M/Sgt Ed Hanley, of the 67th BS groundcrew, and Jean Craig, housekeeper to the Patterson family, who owned the land on which the first USAAF heavy bomber base in Norfolk was constructed.

it be all right if I see you there?' and I simply said 'All right'.

"He came along at 11pm, because he had been on duty. It had been dark when we'd spoken on the road, but as soon as he opened the door I knew it was him and he came straight to me.

"One thing I liked about him was he had a tooth missing, and I thought here's an American who's not so perfect after all. At that time, there was an impression that Americans had everything, money, the lot, but it didn't bother me because I didn't ever look for that. A lot did, though, and I am sure a lot of girls were very unhappy as a result.

"When they got to America they found it wasn't all fun and games, it wasn't all dances and movies. People over there worked hard for what they'd got, harder it seemed to me than over here.

"The dance had been on the Tuesday night, and during our conversation 'Bill' had asked me if I knew where he could buy Christmas cards to send home. We didn't usually have them out at that time of year, but I said I'd ask Miss Clarke, the lady I lived with, if we could put them out in the post office, which we did and he came over on the Thursday. And it took him about three hours to select 12 Christmas cards!

"From then on we started dating. We went to movies and village dances, and we spent many evenings by the fire along with Miss Clarke, who made 'Bill' feel very welcome.

"In the January, I wrote to my parents, telling them about him, and they invited us home for the weekend, and they liked him very much. I felt very comfortable about it, and they did, too, although they knew that if anything did come of this, I'd be leaving.

"Bill was the oldest of seven children, and he had written to his family and had a wonderful letter back from his mother, saying that whatever he decided they would accept and they were wonderful to me.

"On my birthday that year, September 25, we were engaged, and we decided to marry as soon as we could, which turned out to be January 3,

1945, and we were married in Burgh St Peter Methodist Chapel.

"I still lived and worked in Worlingworth, and 'Bill' would come over to stay with us whenever he could. We got to see each other about every other day. We didn't live together or have our own home. We'd been married about 2½ months when 'Bill' was sent over to France."

The end of the war brought no immediate joy to the young couple. 'Bill' arrived home in the United States on their first wedding anniversary, but it was another seven months before Beryl could join him.

"It was a lonely time, but everyone rallied round to help me get there. There were procedures to go through, forms to fill out and mine did not arrive, so I had to go the American Embassy to get them. While there, I saw so many of those girls with loose morals. I hadn't been in contact with that kind of thing before and my aunt, who I was staying with, was very worried that I'd be travelling in that sort of company.

"Eventually we went to a holding camp at Tidworth. It was an army barracks, and we were supposed to be there for three days. But our ship was delayed and we were there for three weeks, before we sailed, all 750 of us brides, from South-ampton."

It had been a deeply distressing time, but at least there was a happy ending to her long wait. Others were not so fortunate.

"My friend had become pregnant by her American boyfriend, and in those cases you could get permission to be married within three days ...So they were married and they were at our wedding as bridesmaid and groom's man. Eventually, he was shipped out and then, when she was on the boat to go over, she was called to the captain's quarters. He told her that her husband had got in touch with them and said he did not want her to come and that he was already married when they'd met."

In 1995, 'Bill' and Beryl Watson celebrated their 50th wedding anniversary with an English tea party in Easley, South Carolina, surrounded by family and friends.

St John's Catholic Church, Norwich, was the setting for the wedding of Captain Edward Israel, who was base technical inspector for the 448th BG at Seething, and Norwich girl Miriam Thorpe.

Sgt James R.Underwood, from Fabius, New York, and his Thetford bride, Freda Newton, run the confetti gauntlet after their wedding on April 8, 1944. Sgt Underwood was serving at East Wretham, a former RAF bomber station which became home to the Mustangs of the 359th Fighter Group and the 448th Air Service Group.

Members of the 100th BG laid on a wedding reception for 'one of their favourite sons' at Brockdish Parish Hall on May 13, 1944. Cpl Ronald William Crider, of the communications section, had just married his sweetheart, Red Cross worker Catherine Drummond, at Thorpe Abbotts Church.

A funny thing happened at the wedding of Cpl Reo Hunt and Joan Moore at St Margaret's Church, Seething, on March 20, 1945, as Walter Stauffer, a fellow member of the 448th BG, relates: "The GIs sat on one side and the local gentry on the other. One of our men was delegated to pump the organ and he picked a solemn moment to sneak a peek from behind the organ. The sight of him peeking around sent us into a burst of giggles, much to the displeasure of the vicar." The vicar, pictured here with the wedding group, was the Revd Donald McClenaghan.

Above and Beyond

THE Medal of Honor, with its star-spangled blue ribbon, is America's highest award for military valour. It is bestowed only on those servicemen who have performed feats of gallantry 'above and beyond the call of duty'. During World War Two only 433 such awards were made, roughly one for every 37,000 men in uniform. Two went to airmen flying out of Norfolk. Both were crew members of a B-17 Flying Fortress based at Deopham Green. This is their story...

Early on the morning of November 9, 1944, Donald Gott's crew were woken to prepare for the 162nd mission of the 452nd Bombardment Group.

In the usual pre-flight ritual, they breakfasted before reporting to the operational briefing where they learned that their squadron, the 729th, would lead the Group's force of 38 bombers and pathfinders.

Their target for the day was the Metz-Thionville German defensive line in eastern France; their task to ease the path of General Patton's Third Army. The secondary target was the Saarbrucken railroad marshalling yards. The mission's emergency landing field was given as the A-72 Airport, near Peronne. The briefing over, the crews filed out to board vehicles which ferried them to their waiting aircraft.

Gott's crew did not have a regular airplane. They had always flown whatever bomber was available. That particular morning they were listed to take B-17G-35VE, serial number *42-97904*. The aircraft had been delivered to the 8th Air Force in England on D-Day, June 6, and someone, somewhere along the way had christened her

The Lady Jeanette — a name she carried, proudly painted on her nose.

For three of the crew, it would be their 27th mission. Although most had been together throughout their tour, some had picked up extra missions and others had fallen behind due to bouts of ill health.

The most experienced man among them was their pilot, 1st Lieut Donald Joseph Gott. Aged 21, Gott, from Arnett, Oklahoma, had already flown 27 missions since joining the 729th Squadron in August and his uniform bore the ribbon of the Air Medal with three oak-leaf clusters.

Alongside him that cold autumn morning was 2nd Lieut William E. Metzger Jr, who had replaced his regular co-pilot. 2nd Lieut Gerald W.Collins had been assigned to another crew to give them an experienced man.

Although a few months older than Gott, Bill Metzger, from Lima, Ohio, had completed only two missions. Nicknamed 'The Reverend' on account of his declared intention to take holy orders prior to joining the USAAF, he had arrived in England in October. According to his younger sister, Metzger had been 'wild about airplanes' and flying since he was a boy.

There was another late replacement aboard *The Lady Jeanette.* 2nd Lieut Joseph F. Harms had been hurriedly drafted in as a substitute for the crew's regular

1st Lieut Donald Joseph Gott, pilot of *The Lady Jeanette*. The mission of November 9, 1944, was his 28th since arriving at Deopham Green in August (USAAF drawing).

bombardier who inexplicably failed to appear — an absence for which he was subsequently court martialled and jailed for a year. Harms had flown only one previous mission.

The rest of the crew consisted of 2nd Lieut John A.Harland, navigator, a native of Chicago with 19 missions under his belt; T/Sgt Russell W.Gustafson, flight engineer and top turret gunner from Oklahoma City; T/Sgt Robert A.Dunlap, radio operator from Miles City, Montana; S/Sgt James O.Fross, belly turret gunner; S/Sgt William R.Robbins, right waist gunner; and S/Sgt Herman B.Krimminger, tail gunner. Gustafson, Dunlap and Fross had all flown 26 missions. Robbins had completed one fewer and Krimminger 22.

Those crewmen embarking on their 27th combat operation had all written home. Their letters talked of a better life to come and spelled out their hopes of being 'home for Christmas' 1944.

Having completed their pre-flight checks, the roar of engines shattered the early morning peace at Deopham Green. At 5.30am, the 38 B-17s climbed into the cloudy sky and head for their assembly point before sweeping out in tight formation across the English coast.

The journey out was uneventful. There was eight-tenths cloud cover en route, which worsened over the target area. The 452nd bombers reached their bombing altitude at 9.13am, but just prior to beginning the run-in, the Group was ordered to divert to its secondary target for a sighted bomb drop.

Just minutes away from the bombing point, flak began to blossom around the B-17s as they flew steadily on at 23,000 feet. 2nd Lieut Collins, normally Gotts' co-pilot,

was piloting a B-17 on the right of the Group formation when he saw, just ahead of him, a flash on the starboard wing of *The Lady Jeanette*. Collins' aircraft rocked under the turbulence of the flak, and as he brought her under control he saw *The Lady Jeanette* flying as No.4 aircraft, leaving formation on a bearing that would take her back towards friendly territory. He called his crew to watch for parachutes, but the B-17 was lost to sight before any were seen.

Aboard *The Lady Jeanette*, T/Sgt Gustafson's turret was facing forward when he heard and felt the flak burst strike the bomber. He swivelled the turret to the right and, to his amazement, saw that the No.4 engine had disappeared — firewall, engine mount and all, clear back to the wing! Immediately, flames billowed out from beneath the wing and trailed past the tail.

It was obvious to Gustafson that the explosion had bent the fuel line and that the gasoline streaming out was responsible for the fire. Swivelling his turret back, he dropped down to tell the pilot what he'd seen. As engineer, it was his job to turn off the fuel supply to the missing engine.

But just as he stepped down to the flight deck, the bomber jolted and twisted under the impact of another flak burst which exploded below Nos 1 and 2 engines, sending shards of razor-sharp shrapnel slicing through the fuselage. Gustafson was hit just above the right ankle, and the same fragment which tore away a large chuck of flesh and bone from his leg careered on to puncture the hydraulic tanks behind the co-pilot. Another fragment ripped

2nd Lieut William Edward Metzger Jr. co-pilot known as 'The Reverend'. He had joined the 452nd BG only the month before his third and final mission (USAAF drawing).

T/Sgt Robert A.Dunlap, radio operator. Seriously wounded by flak, he died when *The Lady Jeanette* exploded as Gott and Metzger made a vain attempt at a crash landing.

through the radio operator's table, severing Robert Dunlap's right hand just above the wrist, and he collapsed with more shrapnel in his leg.

Fross, in the ball turret, already concussed by the first explosion was peppered with fragments of flak from the second burst.

The Lady Jeanette was in a parlous state. No.4 engine had been blown away; No.1 engine had stopped, its propellers locked in the normal flight position and not feathered, which would have cut wind resistance; and No.2 engine was pouring smoke. Inside the fuselage, hydraulic fluid was flooding out of the ruptured tanks on the bomb bay bulkhead, the radio had been knocked out and the intercom was dead.

As the bomber dropped out of formation, Gott and Metzger quickly weighed up their options. They were losing altitude, the bomb bay was open and the bombs were still on board.

Someone had to check out the back and see if the bombs could be kicked free. Gott had to hold the controls. If he let go his grip, the bomber would quickly go into a spin and the crew would be trapped inside due to centrifugal force. But if the aircraft could hang on long enough, they might just be able to make friendly territory near Verdun, site of the titanic World War One struggle between the armies of France and Germany. As *The Lady Jeanette* struggled westwards, Metzger climbed down from his seat. He soon found Gustafson, lying in great pain on the deck, his broken right leg under him.

Several things were happening all at once for the injured engineer. He had tried to

S/Sgt Herman B.Krimminger, tail gunner. He died when his parachute snagged the blazing bomber's tailplane.

T/Sgt Russell Gustafson, engineer. He survived, despite serious leg injuries.

A formation of B-17s from the
452nd BG head out on a mission
from Deopham Green.

inject himself with morphine, but his flying suit was too thick. And, as he struggled to open his suit, he noticed that the flares stored on the bulkhead behind him had started to burn. Then, Metzger emerged from the flight deck. Leaning over, he asked him if he was all right. Gustafson replied that his parachute had been ruined by the leaking hydraulic fluid, and he asked Metzger to bring him the spare 'chute stored in the radio compartment.

Without hesitation, Metzger unclipped his own parachute and gave it to Gustafson. As the co-pilot moved towards the bomb-bay, Gustafson grabbed the burning flare bag and tossed it through the hatch between the pilots' positions towards the forward escape hatch, which the navigator had already jettisoned. Someone, probably Harland, then threw the bag out of the aircraft.

One hazard had been removed, but back

High above Germany, a 452nd BG B-17 comes under fire. There is no known picture of *The Lady Jeanette*. Officially listed as aircraft No.904, the B-17 which has been variously described as *The Lady Janet* and *The Lady Jeanette* was delivered to the USAAF by the Lockheed Corporation of Burbank, California, on April Fool's Day, 1944. According to Russell Gustafson *The Lady Jeanette* was his crew's first permanently assigned aircraft and the sortie of November 9, 1944 was their first and last mission in her.

in the bomb bay, Metzger was struggling in vain to kick the bombs loose. Forced to concede defeat, Metzger moved into the radio compartment, where he found T/Sgt Dunlap passing into shock from loss of blood and pain.

By the time S/Sgt Robbins had helped a concussed and disorientated S/Sgt Fross from the ball turret, they were met by S/Sgt Krimminger, who had come forward from the tail, and together they helped Metzger bind up Dunlap's wounds. Things could hardly have been worse for the stricken bomber. Flames continued to stream past the tail from the starboard wing while a plume of smoke streaked from the port wing. Gott was forced to call on all his flying skills to keep the ship airborne with only one engine producing full power.

Taking the spare 'chute with him, Metzger headed back to the cockpit. By then, the combination of the morphine and pain from his wounds were beginning to take their effect on Gustafson, who says: "I was out of the loop and just sat there hurting.'

Once again, Gott and Metzger conferred. Dunlap's condition was the prime consideration. His only hope lay in swift medical assistance. To parachute him out offered no such certainty. Nor did a crash-landing, even if the bomb-laden aircraft survived impact with the ground. Their best hope, possibly their only real hope, of saving him lay in trying to reach the emergency landing strip near Peronne, but could the burning plane remain airborne long enough?

Many a bomber had crashed with a single engine out, many more with two engines gone. Few had survived more than 1½ hours with the kind of damage The Lady Jeanette had suffered. The strain on the crew was almost unbearable. They faced death at any moment if the bomber lost airspeed and stalled. They faced death in the event of a crash-landing, and, with so little engine control, they faced death even if they succeeded in reaching Peronne.

By then, Dunlap had slipped into unconsciousness.

S/Sgt Robbins remembers: "We were so cover-

ed with Dunlap's blood... that I don't remember Fross having any wounds, but he did still have his leather helmet on which would help hide them. Fross was very disorientated and both Krimminger and I were shook up from the situation. We dumped everything we could and we tried to drop the ball turret. However, we were unable to do so. Later, we gathered near the escape hatch and waited for word to bail out."

According to Gustafson, they struggled on for approximately 1½hrs, with the constant fear that the flames would either reach the fuel tanks or burn through the wing. Luck, however, appeared to be with them. The damaged engine was running roughly, but it kept going along with No.3 engine. Sufficient power was found to keep the aircraft flying above stalling speed. The loss of altitude was a growing concern. It had to be sacrificed to maintain speed. Altitude was their saviour and its loss would be their deaths.

Within 25 minutes of leaving their formation, the bomber crossed over into friendly territory. But Gott and Metzger were experiencing difficulties in controlling the labouring aircraft's course. Still streaming fire and smoke from the starboard wing, The Lady Jeanette skewed to the right. They were flying in a large circle, but they were getting nearer to the emergency landing field.

Some 90 minutes after being struck by flak, they were just ten miles from Peronne and safety. So near and yet so far. They were too far to the north to align on the east-west runway. Their only chance was to reach the northeast-southwest strip. It was time now to get everyone out who could get out. As they banked 45 degrees to line-up for the final approach, word was passed back to bail out.

The first to go was 2nd Lieut Harms, the bombardier, using the forward escape hatch. As he passed, S/Sgt Robbins, who hadn't heard any order, saw his parachute and jumped after him, using the rear escape hatchway. He, in turn, was to be followed out by Krimminger and Fross.

Harms, Robbins and Fross all made safe descents. But disaster overtook the unfortunate

Herman B.Krimminger. His parachute had accidentally opened inside the aircraft, and was snatched by the wind out of the open hatch. As it blew over the plane's horizontal stabiliser, T/Sgt Krimminger was jerked out of the bomber. With his parachute shroud lines wrapped round the tail, he was dragged helpless and flailing in the wind behind the burning aircraft.

Up front, as this tragedy was being played out, Lieut Harland prepared to go and T/Sgt Gustafson, in great discomfort from his broken leg, shuffled along on his backside, through the hatchway between the cockpit and nose compartment, down the steps and along the deck towards the hatch. His last view of the pilots was of Lieut Gott holding firm to the controls and Lieut Metzger assisting.

Years later, Harland would tell his children that Lieut Metzger had given him a parachute as his had been damaged. But for Metzger's selfless act, they would never have been born. Harland jumped, followed by Gustafson.

The last man to exit *The Lady Jeanette*, Gustafson estimated the bomber's height as around 1,500ft. The cold air slapped him in the face.

"My chute opened up into a beautiful white umbrella," he says, "and to this day I do not remember actually pulling the ripcord."

Looking westwards, he watched the aircraft fly on for a few seconds before it started to bank to the left. Moments later, the B-17 rolled over onto its back and dived earthwards. The flames from the ruptured fuel line were sucked into the tanks and the aircraft exploded about 100ft off the ground, the shattered remains continuing to dive straight down.

Upon hitting the ground, the bombs exploded and smoke and flame flashed from the impact point to engulf the wreckage of *The Lady Jeanette.*

As Gustafson drifted earthwards, about half a mile from the crash scene, his only concern was landing with a broken leg.

"Fortunately", he recalls, "the air was heavy, and my descent was slow and I was able to land without further injury.

"After a few minutes on the ground, two Frenchmen came up to me and offered to give aid. Another four or five minutes brought an American ambulance, and I was on my way to a field hospital. The next 12-13 months were spent in army hospitals putting my leg back together. After receiving a medical discharge, I closed the door on the war."

Despite everything, the last flight of *The Lady Jeanette* had ended in tragedy with four men dead; a tragedy relieved only by the splendid courage and self-sacrifice of pilot Donald Gott and co-pilot Bill Metzger.

They had refused to abandon their gravely injured crewman to his fate, electing instead to remain at the controls of their crippled bomber in a desperate attempt to save his life. They did so in the full knowledge that their chances of surviving a crash landing in a burning aircraft with bombs still aboard were virtually nil.

There could be only one reward for such gallantry. A few months later, after the survivors' accounts had been collated, the United States Government announced the posthumous awards of the Medal of Honor to Donald J.Gott and William E.Metzger Jr.

Each citation concluded with the words: "(His) loyalty to his crew, his determination to accomplish the task set forth to him, and his deed of knowingly performing what may have been his last service to his country was an example of valor at its highest."

One man, at least, was not surprised by the courage displayed by the young stand-in co-pilot flying only his third combat mission. Harold Burrell had flown as a member of Bill Metzger's original crew, and years later he recalled Metzger assuring them that 'he would never leave a wounded crew member on board'.

He had kept his promise at the cost of his life.

(Adapted from *The Last Flight of The Lady Jeanette* by Willis S.Cole Jr with additional information supplied by T/Sgt Russell Gustafson).

Russell Gustafson and Mayor Madame Giselle-Maire Fronnier unveil *The Lady Jeanette* memorial at Tincourt-Boucly, in France, on the 50th anniversary of the mission.

A close-up view of the memorial.

Peace at Last

FIREWORKS, flares and a fusillade of gunfire heralded the arrival of VE Day at US air-bases throughout Norfolk. The announcement of Germany's unconditional surrender had long been expected. Rumours were rife and a formal declaration was widely expected on May 7.

In the event, VE Day was declared 24 hours later. Long before the official speeches began, however, the celebrations were under way. And for some they were to prove almost as hazardous as the war itself!

The unit diarist of the 715th Squadron based at Seething describes the unfortunate fate of one Flying Officer Barilla: "Even though VE Day was May 8, F/O Barilla...decided to do a bit of celebrating on the night before. He landed in hospital with a .45 calibre slug through his hand."

That there were not any fatalities at some bases was something of a minor miracle.

Joseph D.Roure, of the 93rd BG based at Hardwick, had completed 14 missions by the end of the war and he reckons VE Day in Norfolk proved almost as dangerous as any of those sorties over Germany.

"One of the first things that happened," he recalls, "was that all the trash-barrels in our hut area were set afire, and all the waste-paper, scrap lumber and other inflammables that could be found were fed to the flames. This was sane enough, but apparently a little too tame for some of our more high-spirited lads, who then began to dig out the souvenir caliber .50 shells and .45 ammunition that had been collected during their tours as well as any that might have been left behind by departing warriors.

At Watton, the simple headline on the US forces newspaper, *Stars and Stripes*, tells its own story of VE Day, as a local policeman gets in on the act.

The control tower, revellers and Liberators are silhouetted as flares shoot up in the sky above Seething to celebrate the end of the war.

The partying continued throughout May 8, with local girls and Red Cross workers joining in the fun at the Seething base hospital.

"It turned out to be a sizeable cache of mixed cartridges that were tossed by the handful into the blazing GI cans. In a few seconds they had heated sufficiently to detonate, many of the slugs penetrating the sides of the cans and flying about on random trajectories. It was soon not worth one's life to venture out in the area …As if that were not enough, a couple of other bright chaps remembered a Very (signalling) pistol that some-one had scrounged …along with a supply of star shells. Before long, there were colored balls of light arching over and around the huts. And that reminded somebody in a nearby Nissen that they, too, knew where another Very gun, with its flares, was stashed. The predictable outcome was a colorful, if somewhat precarious, 'battle' between the huts involved, until all the shells were exhausted. Thankfully, we never heard of any but the most casual injuries sustained during these wild antics…"

Many likened the pyrotechnic displays to Fourth of July celebrations back home.

Bert J.La Point III, who had spent 22 months with the 448th BG, reckons that the flares 'lit up the sky like I had never seen it lit up'.

He writes: 'I think that more flares were shot off that night than through all the time we were there.'

Yet amid the uproarious partying there was an element of sadness for some. Pat Everson, then a girl of ten whose home bordered the Seething airbase, remembers watching the flares turning night into day: "As a young schoolgirl I could not remember fireworks; usually if any lights were seen in the sky or bangs heard it was something to do with searchlights or guns. My mother explained that the war was over and that they were celebrating this, and also that they would soon be returning to America. I remember sitting at the bedroom windows crying as I did not want

A colour party from the USAAF Military Police leads the way.

them to leave. They had brought colour and excitement to the children around the base..."

But even for the men celebrating there was, in some cases at least, a final price to be paid.

Peace or no peace, senior officers at Seething were not prepared to allow the unauthorised use of carbines and pistols to go unpunished. According to Captain Edmer J.Lacasse, 712th Squadron adjutant at Seething: "This resulted in all the officers getting up at 5am the next morning for a march around the perimeter."

It was, it must be said, one of the most sobering starts to the real VE Day...

The Grand Parade

IT was a day of pomp and circumstance to rank alongside the most glittering occasions in the county's long history. The grand Victory Parade through the crowd-lined streets of Norwich on

Sunday, May 13, 1945, was a day to remember — a day of pride and thanksgiving.

But more than anything, it was a glorious reflection of the bond of friendship forged between Britain and the United States in the heat of war.

Sharing the saluting platform outside a flag-bedecked City Hall with Field Marshal Lord Ironside was Brigadier-General Leon Johnson, the highly-decorated commander of the Ship-dham-based *Flying Eightballs* 44th BG.

And alongside the British and Imperial troops marching past with colours flying and bands playing were the servicemen and women of the 8th USAAF.

According to the *EDP:* 'Every window overlooking the route and every accessible vantage point was occupied. The top of one market stall partially subsided just before the parade amid general amusement...'

Eyes right as units from nearby air bases march past City Hall with the ancient Guildhall behind them.

Crowds line the walk to cheer an impressive motorcade of white-helmeted American military policemen along Gentleman's Walk. Note the banner advertising a Grand Victory Ball at the Samson and Hercules on Wednesday, May 16.

Among the Americans who took part that day was Robert S.Lawson, the commander of 1132nd Quartermaster Company, based at Shipdham.

He remembers: "I was supposed to march at the head of my company, but when we assembled I was snatched away from my friends of the past four years and assigned to lead another unit. We started off by falling behind an American unit and I became conscious of the cheers becoming louder and louder. The warm, friendly British crowd, after six years of suffering, were cheering us! I believe we should have been cheering them. About a block away from City Hall, the striking lions in front of the building became visible — beautiful sculpture, Delosiam probably. I turned untraditionally and shouted to my troops, 'C'mon fellows, walk proud and make it look good for the general'...Memories may fade but the 50 years affiliation of America and England — allies and friends — will always endure."

Taking the salute was Brigadier General Leon Johnson, CO at Shipdham, a holder of the Congressional Medal of Honor and a legendary figure within the USAAF.

Every vantage point was taken over as the crowds flocked into the city to see the parade.

Afterwards, the servicemen and women of both nations joined together for a Service of Thanksgiving in Norwich Cathedral.

A Hero Called Leon

WHEN the city of Norwich staged its grand victory parade in May 1945, the honour of taking the salute on the steps of the City Hall was shared by senior officers reflecting the great Anglo-American alliance.

Field Marshal Lord Ironside, a distinguished Norfolk-domiciled soldier whose career spanned two world wars, represented Britain's armed forces.

Alongside him stood a 40-year-old USAAF officer who had come to epitomise the courageous resolution displayed by thousands of his fellow countrymen during the relentless aerial offensive waged from the fields of East Anglia. His name was Brigadier General Leon W.Johnson.

Highly respected and hugely popular, he had commanded the 44th Bomb Group, the famed *Flying Eightballs* of Shipdham, earning almost every honour his country could bestow.

His awards were headed by the Medal of Honor, the American equivalent of the Victoria Cross. He had won it for his gallant leadership during the audacious and costly low-level bombing attack on the heavily-defended Rumanian oilfields at Ploesti on August 1, 1943 which was mounted from airstrips in North Africa.

The medal was presented to him at Shipdham

Early days in Norfolk. Col Leon Johnson finds a seat on a pile of corrugated roofing amid the mud and snow. Johnson was among the first staff officers from the Eighth Air Force to arrive in the UK in the summer of 1942. He assumed command of the 44th BG at Shipdham in January 1943.

amid much pomp and publicity in the following autumn. It was the only ceremony of its kind to be staged in Norfolk during the war. Johnson continued to lead from the front, and it was always reckoned by his men that the more hazardous the mission, the more likely his would be the first name on the operational crew list.

Such inspirational leadership had a great effect on the 44th BG and the whole of the 14th Combat Wing. Col Edward K.Mikoloski, who served on his staff at Shipdham, recalls how 50 years after the war a member of his original crew had remarked that 'he and the rest of the crew would follow the General on any mission as long as he directed it'.

He then added: "Even now, if he told me to jump off the Empire State Building, I would — in full confidence that I would survive the jump!"

Andy Rooney, a wartime journalist with the *Stars and Stripes* newspaper, was effusive in his praise of Johnson. He remembered him as a 'good commander, good pilot and all-around regular guy'.

A naturally self-effacing man, Johnson was unaffected by his fame. Despite his seniority and his many honours he mixed easily with men of all ranks.

Mikoloski remembers: "Johnson would always stop and share his staff car with the

Low level to Ploesti. Photographs of 44th BG Liberators led by Leon Johnson during one of the most famous raids of the war. Finding his Group's objective at the Rumanian oil refinery complex already on fire, Johnson switched to a different target. Of 177 B-4s which took part in *Operation Tidal Wave,* 54 were lost, including 11 from the 44th. Recalling the raid, Johnson remarked: "It was more like an artist's impression of an air-battle than anything I had ever experienced. We flew through sheets of flame, and airplanes were everywhere, some of them on fire and others exploding. It's indescribable to anyone who wasn't there."

airmen, taking them into Norwich or East Dereham. He reportedly always stopped at the 'Big Tree' on the Base and filled his car with airmen going into town."

One of Mikoloski's abiding memories of Johnson, however, revealed another side of his character: "While at the 14th Combat Wing in December 1943, the General came to my quarters with the staff Chaplain. He took it upon himself to convey to me the news of the sudden death of my infant son, who was born in June 1943 during my tour in the UK. The tragic news was a shock and heart-breaker to me and without much thought I broke down and cried.

"The General comforted me as best as one could under the circumstances and asked if I preferred to be alone. I did not respond as the sobbing continued unabated. When I finally got myself under control (the General never did leave) I apologised for losing control...He put his hand on my shoulder and said, 'Mike, you don't need to apologise under these circumstances. And anyway, I've always felt and said, "Show me a man who will cry and I'll show you a man." Later that evening, after dinner, he came to see me again and asked if I wanted to go home on emergency leave. When I responded that I would, but that at this time of the war getting back would be difficult, he said, 'Why don't you act as a courier and take the Medal of Honor to the US for me?'

"I did take his medal to the US and personally delivered it to his wife and two daughters in Savannah, Georgia. My wife accompanied me and that gesture did provide us some relief from the grief we were suffering with the loss of our son. With all the responsibilities the General was carrying at that time with the war, the mission planning and the expansion of our forces coming into the UK, he took the time and made the

Distinguished gathering at Shipdham, June 1943. Taking tea with Leon Johnson, right, is Lieut General Jacob Devers. Note the *Flying Eightball* wall art.

Honour parade. Leon Johnson receives the Medal of Honor, America's highest gallantry award, in front of the control tower at Shipdham on November 22, 1943. The presentation, in front of officers and men of the 44th BG, was made by Lieut Gen Jacob Devers. By the end of the war, Johnson's list of decorations would include the Silver Star, Legion of Merit, Distinguished Flying Cross, Air Medal and the British DFC.

Shipdham played host to a local civic dignatory on January 20, 1944. Leon Johnson had been promoted to Brigadier-General in command of the 14th Wing the previous September. He is seen here, alongside his distinguished visitor, in the cockpit of a veteran B-24.

Leon Johnson talking with a 44th BG crew at Shipdham.

effort to console and comfort a member of his staff."

Leon Johnson's connections with Norfolk were to continue after the war when, as commander of the 3rd Air Force he played a prominent role in establishing Sculthorpe as one of America's main UK bases. Now in his 90s, he is president of the 44th BG Veterans Association and, according to Mikoloski, his affection for the British people remains undimmed:

"His most frequently used statement at the closing of his many speeches was 'Freedom is a God-given right but freedom is not a God-guaranteed right. It must be nourished, it must be protected. Freedom is everybody's business.' The outstanding symbol of that philosophy, he stated, were the valiant people of England, who endured much adversity during and after the war. He instilled his troops with that respect and admiration for the English people, and, in my estimation, that accounts greatly for the close relationships that were developed between us and the fine people around Norwich and the Norfolk area."

Memories

Michael Downs
Wortwell

"I was born in 1936, so by 1942, I was at an impressionable age. My first inkling that something big was going to happen was when lorry after lorry came passing through Attleborough, where I lived, loaded with sand and ballast. They were building the 'dromes' as we called them. My father came home from work one day and said: 'The Yanks are coming today,' so he rigged up a seat on the crossbar of his bicycle and rode me down to Snetterton Heath.

"We waited and in they came — the planes — all painted khaki. Within a matter of months, we had five different air bases within a radius of five to six miles. After a couple of days, the Americans were let out for the first time. They came by our house in hundreds! One man was wearing Texan cowboy boots and shouted to me that he was The Lone-Star Ranger, at which I ran indoors to tell my parents — I really believed him!

"In no time at all, we kids were chewing gum and eating candy (a real luxury for us). Lots of airmen used to ask if I had a sister. 'Yes', I would say. 'How old?' they would ask. 'Well, she's eight or nine or ten," I'd tell them, depending on which period of the war I was asked. At the time I couldn't understand why their enthusiasm waned when I told them her age.

"We boys soon had our own 'Yank' friend. Mine was a man called 'George' who came from New Jersey. He was a waist gunner in a Flying Fortress. I would come straight out of school, into the camp, right past the MPs, who waved me through, and on into his hut, or I waited for his plane to land and he would take me to the PX (the US equivalent of the NAAFI). I was given coffee and doughnuts. Both of these were welcome to me.

"I was also given razor blades, chewing gum, candles, etc. When I arrived back home, my father was most annoyed and would tell me: 'No more scrounging!' I kept saying I didn't ask for anything, but from then on the PX was out of bounds for me.

"However, my visits to the airfield continued until the end of the war. I was allowed rides in the aircraft when they were ground tested around the perimeter track. One day my pal did not come back. All his kit had been moved out. I found out later that his plane was shot down over Brunswick. To this day, I do not know whether he survived. He was a very kind man. Of course, I made other American pals, but it was never quite the same."

David Hastings
Salhouse

"My first meeting with the men of the 2nd Air Division, USAAF, came in January 1944 when, as an aviation-mad young schoolboy, word swept through my school in Norwich that Americans were coming to Horsham St Faith. Two of us played truant to watch the Liberators coming in to land over the Cromer Road.

"We waited at the main gate for hours that day to get our first sight of a real American and were rewarded when eventually a whole group of airmen poured out. We admired their smart uniforms, their laughter and friendship and one gave me a silver quarter which I still have today. The next day we received a caning from the headmaster at school for being absent, but it was worth it.

"We spent many happy hours at Horsham until someone told us that the Liberators had arrived at Rackheath and you could get close to their dispersals. Three of us cycled out there and began our association with the 467th. Sadly for us, although the ground crew were friendly, the MPs were not and having been caught for the third time in a B-24, our meeting with the famous Colonel Al Shower scared us all so badly that we decided we had better cycle elsewhere...

"We turned our eyes south and there was Hethel, only 30 minutes hard cycling from where we lived in Norwich. June 1944 saw the

Lieut Al Dexter, second left on the back row, together with the crew of *Pugnacious Princess Pat* at Hethel in 1944.

beginning of the school holidays and we cycled out. Luckily, we found a hardstand close to the back road. The Liberator was away on a mission, but the crew chief, 'Pop' Ganness, made us welcome and suggested we stay to meet his crew. We waited, enjoyed our taste of Coke and were overjoyed at the ground crew's friendship.

"In the late afternoon the sky was filled with the sound of returning Liberators as the Group swept over the field and peeled off to land. Then, a silver B-24 called *Pugnacious Princess Pat* swung into our dispersal, turned around and shut down. The pilot walked over to meet us and so began our friendship with Lieut Al Dexter, the crew of the *Pat* and the 389th Bomb Group. Lieut Dexter lifted me over the fence and introduced me to his crew and then, as usual, the MPs arrived and Al offered them three choices: They could shoot him, which he doubted. They could confine him to barracks, which would be great as he would not have to fly more missions. Or they could get the hell out of there. They left!

"All our school holidays were spent at Hethel. We saw them go out and counted them back. Al Dexter would always walk me around the aircraft on his return, with his hand on my shoulder, pointing out the battle damage (something we realised 50 years later was a crew 'good luck' superstition) and then, after the crew had left, came the great bonus of collecting all the waxed cartons of candies.

"On the days when the crew were not flying, 'Pop' used to smuggle us on board, and, with the put-put running and the intercom on, we flew the *Pat* all over Europe in our imagination.

"We also shared the sadness when crews we had met did not return, but luckily for us Al and his crew completed their 35 missions. Al Dexter and the crew also visited our home in Norwich, where we had 'open house' for the 2nd Air Division, as my mother was Deputy Commandant of the Red Cross, which ran the American Services Club, in the city.

"In November, Al and his crew completed

their tour. We presented them with a wooden model of the *Pat*. Ganness volunteered for air crew, and then the *Pat* and her crew were lost over Germany and it was never quite the same, despite the exciting times. But who can ever forget the sight and sound as hundreds of B-24s slowly assembled over Norwich each day before heading out for Germany?

"Then, in 1945, it was all over. We heard they were leaving, but our school exams kept us away from the airfield for a week or so. When we next cycled out, it was unbelievable. All the Liberators had gone and there was no guard on the main gate. We decided to chance going in and wandered through the empty huts, including Al Dexter's, where copies of *Yank* still lay on the tables. We visited the deserted mess hall where we had enjoyed so many great meals, then the tower and the locked hangars, collecting an American steel helmet on the way. It all seemed impossible, and for the day we had the base to ourselves, even cycling at speed down the main runway. However, the sadness that our American friends had gone was deeply felt indeed."

Pam Prior
Attleborough

"I was a student at Norwich Training College from 1944 to 1946. We had a wonderful principal who thought that the Americans should meet 'decent' girls and so the GIs were invited to the termly college dances. These were great events in our lives and for weeks after most of us had a GI boyfriend and that meant lots of candy, dinner at the Castle Hotel, visits to the Theatre Royal, the Hippodrome and all the Norwich cinemas. They were allowed to visit us in our rooms until 10pm on certain evenings.

"Also, they sent out their Liberty trucks to transport us to their camp dances. These were chaperoned by our senior year students and once there, NO ONE was allowed to leave the dance hall. The spread of food laid out for us was out of this world and how we gorged. I was 18 at the time and enjoyed their company. I was surprised

to learn, years after that, they were considered 'over-sexed'.

"I was friendly with a young man from Colorado until the end of the war. He was good company and a perfect gentleman. I cried buckets when he left and, although I wrote he did not. He and his pals never spoke of what they did. In recent years, when I saw the film *Memphis Belle*, I was appalled at what they had had to do, and longed to be able to tell some of them that I wished I had known at the time.

"We were also invited to the dances at the American Red Cross in the Cellars in King Street. Again, we were escorted there and back by senior students. We walked from College Road, through the centre of Norwich in the blackout and didn't feel in the least afraid or threatened.

"A girl in my hostel was given a Purple Heart by her GI. When she lost touch with him — we didn't know if he had been killed — she felt she should somehow return it. I went with her to the American Red Cross and we were passed from one official to another until we stood before a rather stern man in uniform. He wrote down details and took the Heart, and that was that.

"My second year in college after the Yanks had gone back seemed humdrum. Looking back, I am glad to have known them — their accents, their vitality and their confidence were so different from the village boys I had known, and to this day I think fondly of them.

Ethel Powell
New Buckenham

"My father, Arthur Rush, was licensee of the Wine Cellars pub, New Buckenham, during the war. As it was a free house, he was able to purchase beer from any brewery in the district. Americans stationed at Snetterton and Old Buckenham were frequent visitors. On one occasion when the Americans were confined to their stations, one did manage to slip through a barrier and went to the Wine Cellars. My father was extremely worried, but gave him a drink and told him to go back to his base. But in the meantime, American military police were visiting the George Hotel and the King's Head. Rather than let him get into trouble my father put him in the coal cellar. The police arrived, looked in the bar and rooms and then left. Bringing the American out of the coal cellar, my father pointed him on his way and was thanked profusely."

Eric Jarrold
Norwich

I was 15, and a member of the Air Training Corps, when the Americans arrived in Norfolk. As a member of the ATC, I had a number of visits to USAAF bases, but my last visit to Hethel, on November 12, 1944, was the best of all. We were collected by army lorry as usual from the City of Norwich School, Eaton Road. We were taken to the briefing room at Hethel and given a resumé of the day's itinerary. As we made our way to the control tower, three or four of us slipped away and went to the operations room to see if any Liberators were flying that day.

"We were told that a B-24J (No.0-085) had had an engine change and was to be test flown that morning. We were introduced to the two pilots, issued with chest parachutes and told to wait outside the nearby crew room. We all piled into jeeps and went with the crew to the dispersal point. We flew for about an hour around the city and the base in occasional cloud at 1,000ft. We sat in the various turrets and took turns at sitting in the co-pilot's seat, flying hands on with the pilot giving a commentary as he flew the aircraft. After landing, we went to the mess, had a good lunch and were told if we wanted to go again to go out to the jeeps.

"We flew in the same Liberator again for almost three hours. This time we covered a much larger area, from Cromer in the north to Harwich in the south. We couldn't fly over Yarmouth, Lowestoft or Felixstowe as all aircraft flying over these areas were automatically fired upon. It was almost dark when we landed and after handing in our parachutes we warmly thanked the crews for allowing us to 'unofficially' fly with them.

"My final visit to Horsham St Faith was on April 1, 1945. I was met by USAAF chaplain, Capt Edwards. The first stop was the ground crews' mess. Afterwards, we went on our cycles, visiting the church at the base, the control tower, where we watched Liberators taking off and landing, the Met section and the Air Sea Rescue section. After cycling to the flarepath caravan on the Hellesdon end of the runway 05, I was allowed to flash a green on the Aldis lamp to signal a Liberator to take off. It was a perfect end to 'visiting the USAAF' in wartime Norfolk..."

Dick Wickham
Harleston

"The Clubmobile was run by the American Red Cross. It was a converted London Transport single-decker bus. The driver was English and it was manned by two American girls. Its role was to visit the American Air Force bases and supply doughnuts, coffee, candy and cigarettes to the personnel on the bases, free of charge I might add.

"My connection with the Clubmobile was that one of these buses was based at Harleston where I was living during the war. I had a job on it after school hours — to clean out the coffee urns and make the doughnuts, all ready for the next day's trip...Being rationed as we were for sugar, to see all the sugar that was used to 'dunk' the doughnuts in was something else. All the doughnuts had to be put into racks and stored in built-in cupboards.

"The destination boards at the front and rear of the bus were made into speakers, the music broadcast from these coming from a gramophone inside. A small lounge was situated at the rear, where the two ladies rested while travelling to and from the bases. The bus was stationed at the rear of the Swan Hotel, and the driver and young ladies lived in the hotel itself...Two of us boys were employed, working on the bus, and we were paid seven shillings a week, a lot of money to us. Not only that but we could eat as many doughnuts as we wanted!

"Being mad on aircraft, an added bonus for me

Two American Red Cross girls who manned the Clubmobile, otherwise known as the coffee and doughnut wagon, at Hardwick.

was that at weekends we could travel around the bases and talk to my heroes, the aircrews, and get close to the aircraft...Every time I see those doughnut-making machines working, especially at air shows, memories flood back to me."

Jennifer Hubbard
Norwich

"Early in 1943, Jennifer Bettison, as I then was, had just turned 14 and had started work at Messrs Yules, the drapers in High Street, Dereham. I had left my cycle, my pride and joy, an almost new black and red Raleigh that my parents had bought for me at the back of the shop, but was devastated to find it missing when I left work at 5.30 one afternoon.

"Mr Yule rang the local police who took details, but it still meant a long walk home to Toftwood. Not long after that the police informed me that my cycle had been found at the USAAF base at Shipdham and that I should be

required to give evidence at the base as the culprit had been found and would be dealt with under American military law. I was later collected in a military vehicle — a great adventure — together with Mr Adams, the owner of the local cycle shop, who was to give evidence that he recognised the cycle which he had sold to my family.

"We were driven rapidly through the camp to the building where the investigation was to take place. Far from being an informal matter, as one might have expected from the Americans, it seemed to me, an impressionable teenager, that it could almost have been a murder trial, and this was confirmed when I was quite sharply (and rightly) reprimanded by the presiding officer for giggling during the proceedings. I know that the airman was found guilty, but we were not allowed to stay for his punishment to be disclosed.

"The best part, however, was yet to come; we were taken to a canteen and invited to help ourselves from the apparent mountains of food on display. There was more meat than I had ever seen and fruit in abundance. I had a healthy appetite in those days and took full advantage of the treats on offer. When even I had had enough, there was also a bag of food to take home, and being reunited with my cycle again meant that it had been a memorable day."

Forrest S.Clark
44th BG, Shipdham 1943-45

"When we first arrived at Shipdham base in 1943, it was cold and a damp fog clung to the land and obscured the runways. The first thing I recall on arrival was checking into our squadron living site and the hut which was to be home for the next year or more.

"I noticed that someone was cutting off a

piece of the beams in the hut to make fire wood. In the next few days a contingent of men from the 44th set out to cut some wood from a nearby forest...About two days later, a constable showed up at the squadron living quarters and asked to see the men who had cut down the wood. Unbeknown to the American airmen the wood was the property of the Crown...Taking anything from such property was forbidden.

"The detail of men were called forward to explain, and, of course, their own defence was an ignorance of the law...After some anxious moments of explanation and promises not to do it again, the constable appeared satisfied and departed without further action.

"Needless to say the quarters did receive a ration of coal for the fires, but I recall, as I am sure all others do, the dampness of the floors. We all, or most of us, wore warm socks even in bed...Yet the dampness seeped into the quarters and into the beds and the wind rattled against the huts..."

**Pamela Standley,
Wymondham**
"All of the local girls were able to go to dances on the bases. They would send trucks into the town,

picking us up at the Market Place. Deopham Green was the venue for Wednesday evenings and, sometimes as we arrived at the base, the B-17s would still be returning from that day's raid...I think it brought home to even the flightiest of us the seriousness of what was going on around us.

"These dances were great fun. Usually held in a big hangar, there was a bar and good bands, and I think I can say a good time was had by all...The crews who used to come to our dances enjoyed themselves, but very often they would arrive with some of the familiar faces missing and sometimes whole crews just disappeared. We never talked of this. We knew what had happened...

"Being surrounded by bases...we were very conscious of all these planes taking off in the mornings...we would watch as they circled, quite low at first and then higher and higher, finally forming up and heading off eastwards. It was quite different when they came back. Sometimes a squadron all together, but often just ones and twos. We could tell what sort of mission it had been by the way they returned. And if you had a special boyfriend it all seemed very close. You almost felt part of their lives."

Kaleidoscope

"The sky was always full of aircraft," is an oft-repeated but accurate comment by anyone who lived through the latter half of the war in Norfolk. This photograph shows Liberators from the 44th Bombardment Group 'buzzing' Hardwick airfield, home of the 93rd BG, during low-level training for the audacious raid on the Rumanian oilfields at Ploesti six weeks later. It was during this period that a 44th BG crew chief was heard to comment: "I don't know if I'm crewing a B-24 or a bloody four-engined Spitfire."

Flying Fortresses from the 452nd BG, based at Deopham Green, are stacked up in the clear blue sky as they head out on a mission.

Seen from the ground. A formation of B-17s pass over Wolverton Hall, home of Lord and Lady Walpole, in 1944. The photograph was taken by the present Lord Walpole's father on a German camera captured in the Western Desert.

April 1945 and B-17s of the 452nd BG break formation to land at Deopham Green with the Stars and Stripes at half-mast as a mark of respect to President Franklin D.Roosevelt, whose death had just been announced.

Mission parties are generally remembered for their high-spirited celebrations, but here is proof that there was a serious side to these milestones. The colour party of the 389th BG leads the official parade to mark the Group's 200th mission at Hethel on September 21, 1944.

Wall art was a genre in which USAAF painters excelled. This example was found at Deopham Green.

They were equally famed for the stunning nose art which came to adorn so many of their bombers. *Dumbo* was flown over to Britain by Lieut Delbert Mann, a future Oscar-winning director. His wife, Ann, came up with the name after finding a picture of the Disney elephant in *Life* magazine. Mann never flew the aircraft operationally. On arrival in Britain, he was assigned as a replacement crew to the 467th BG at Rackheath, where he flew 35 missions before being posted as Intelligence Officer to the 491st BG. *Dumbo* went into a pool of replacement planes and eventually ended up with the 453rd BG at Old Buckenham. She completed 77 missions, surviving severe damage during a raid on Kassel in September 1944, to fly again. She is seen here at Old Buckenham with 735th Squadron Engineering Officer Harry Godges alongside.

Nose art was taken a stage further with this particular B-17, which flew out of Snetterton as part of the 96th BG. *5 Grand*, the 5,000th Fortress built by Boeing at Seattle, was autographed by all the workers in the company's plant. She arrived at Snetterton in 1944, completed 78 missions and was flown back to the States where she ended her days in the Arizona desert. The city of Seattle had wanted to purchase her as a permanent memorial, but by the time they decided to act it was too late. *5 Grand* had been scrapped!

Taking it lying down. A waist gunner from Capt Bill Brandon's 66th Bomb Squadron crew has a doze on the edge of the runway at Shipdham while waiting for a mission.

They also served. A shot of the Women's Army Corps basketball team from Ketteringham Hall, headquarters of the 2nd Air Division, who were crowned divisional champions in 1945.

Cartoon commentary on the results of the Anglo-American relationship.

Airmen from the 452nd BG at Deopham Green inspect the wreckage of a V1 which came down in a field near the base. It may be from the 'buzz bomb' that Sgt Kenneth R.Berkheimer spotted streaking across the base one frosty, moonlit night: "Just as the V1 was directly overhead, it went 'burrip' and shut off. There was an unearthly silence as we waited for it to crash its 1,000lb warhead in our vicinity. It finally plunged into a farmer's field about half a mile away with a mighty roar, flash and earth movement. Everyone either returned to their sack as mad as hell or, in our case, we went to fly a long mission. That was close!"

Aircraft were not the only pieces of military hardware on USAAF bases in Norfolk to be christened after popular females. Helen Malstead, American Red Cross programme director with the 392nd BG at Wendling, had one of the base defence armoured cars named *Helen's Happy ARC Warriors* in her honour at a special ceremony on September 10, 1944.

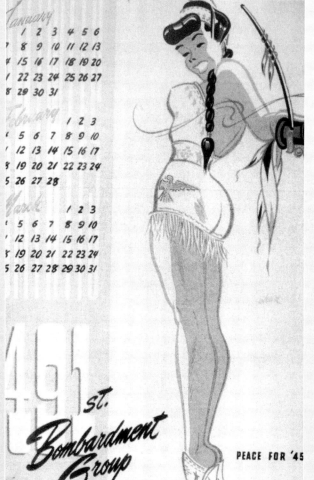

A typical piece of home-produced artwork. This example adorned a 491st BG calendar at North Pickenham.

Act of Remembrance

IT IS a little piece of England that is forever a part of America. The glorious stained-glass window at the 12th-century St Andrew's Church, Quidenham, is the shining symbol of the 8th Air Force's oldest and arguably most evocative memorial in Britain.

St Mary's Chapel is dedicated to the memory of those men from the 96th Bombardment Group who made the ultimate sacrifice while flying out of the nearby Snetterton Heath airbase. With its lone airman, in flying suit, looking up towards the figure of Christ while a group of Flying Fortresses assemble high in the clouds above the spire of St Andrew's, the window paints a powerful image of the heavy price paid for victory.

The impressive memorial was officially unveiled and dedicated by the Bishop of Norwich, the Rt Revd Percy Herbert, in November 1944, at the height of the bombing campaign. It had its roots, however, in an association forged by the Revd William Harper-Mitchell. A number of Americans were married in the church and servicemen became regular members of the congregation.

The first thoughts on a lasting memorial were expressed by Captain Herbert Allen, surgeon of the 338th Squadron, in April 1944. The idea won the enthusiastic backing of his unit's executive officer, Captain Robert L.Robb, who agreed to lead a fund-raising campaign, and the Base Chaplain, Charles K.Smith. A preliminary design for the window was made by Sgt Gerald Athey, a crew chief from 413th Squadron, and this was exhibited in the Officers' Club, the Non-Coms' Club and the Aeroclub. With the whole-hearted support of the Revd Harper-Mitchell and the

Evolution of a lasting memorial. The cross and candlesticks take shape in Norwich with the Revd William Harper Mitchell, artist Reginald Bell and the Group Adjutant, Col Sandy Moffatt inspecting the work.

Local people join with American servicemen for the dedication service at St Andrew's Church, Quidenham, in November 1944.

Sgt Gerald Athey, the man whose original design was accepted for the memorial window.

The oldest memorial to the 8th Air Force in Britain honours the men of the 96th BG who did not return home. The 96th suffered the second-highest loss rate in the Mighty Eighth.

War artist Frank Beresford painting his famous portrait of an airman praying in St Mary's Chapel. In fact, the figure was posed by local man Tony Green, who happened to be working in the churchyard at the time Beresford arrived.

The artist Reginald Bell, whose stained-glass work distinguished Yale University Library, the Cathedral of St John the Divine in New York, and Norwich Cathedral, undertook to produce the memorial window, and his final design remained true to Sgt Athey's original model.

Special permission was needed to go ahead with the work because the overall cost of £597 exceeded the amount allowed to be spent on work deemed to be non-essential.

Collection boxes were set up church authorities, the project was extended to and tannoy announcements made across the include the restoration of St Mary's Chapel, com- base, and by Remembrance Sunday 1944, all was plete with altar, candlesticks, cross and mem- ready for the official dedication. orial book.

Farewell to Arms

At Horsham St Faith, a small crowd of local people gather to wave farewell to a Liberator of the 458th BG as it prepares to head back to the United States at the war's end. Although almost certainly posed, it reflects the end of an era in the history of the grand alliance. As events were quickly to prove, however, a new association was about to begin.

Last of the many. Alice Bingham was in her nightgown when she captured this dawn shot of a 458th BG B-24 leaving Horsham St Faith for the last time and flying over Pinewood Close on its way home. She remembers how, earlier in the war, a Liberator crashed partly through her garden and flattened a nearby house: "In those days, we had coal fires and the undercarriage wheels used to cut through the smoke as they flew low over our roofs."

Subscribers

Mrs J C Abbot
Jeff Abbott
Gail Adcock (TSGT R S Russell, 25th Bomb Group)
James Armstrong, Lieut Colonel, US Air Force (Ret)
Chris C Atherton

Elsie Barber
Elsie J Barber
Katie Barber
Robert J B Barker
Mrs Betty Barrett
R N Barrett
Raymond E Beales
P J Beckham
Derek Berry
Mrs J Berwick
Mrs Alice Eva Bingham
Gordon Bixby
William R Bowhill
Mr & Mrs D Bowman
Ann & Pat Bradbury
Richard James Brady
Louise Brighton
Mr P F Brock
Victor R Brockwell
Mr Patrick Brooks
L F Browne
Carol Buck
Derek W J Burroughs
Mr D Burton
Leonard Charles Butcher
Gordon W Butler

Michael R Calver
Mr & Mrs Tom Campana (USA)
Mr D R Carter
Mr & Mrs D Catling
B M F Chapman
Andrew Clayson, Bismarck, North Dakota, USA
Evelyn G Codman
Rex A Coe
Evelyn Cohen
Arthur Colbourn

A J Coleman
Mrs E E Collins
D Collinson
V Cork
P Crawford
Alec B Curtis

Robert W Dance
Mr C W Davey
John I P Davis
Mrs Anne Day
D J Deacon
Mr & Mrs Al Dexter
Barbara Jean Drake
B R P Dunham
Mr & Mrs Joe Dzenowagis

Mrs Phyllis Earrye
Tim East
Mr B Eastaugh
Basil V Eastaugh
Mr Michael Easter
James A Easton
L Robert Einheuser

Marlene Fickling
John W Fincham
Mr R Flatt
R E & J D Flowerdew
Alan Forman
S Foster
Peter R Francis
David Fulcher

Emerald Mary Gaul
Roger Gibbons
Mrs J H Gibbs
Mike Gibbs
Roger K Goodall
Roy C Gough
E W Gowing
Gordon Graham
Mr Glenn Greenwood
Mr & Mrs Geoff Gregory
Mrs D Grint
David Richard Gubbin
Joyce Gurney-Read

Mr Trevor Charles Hadingham
Barry Halford
Alan Hall
Neil Hammond
Mrs Stella Hammond
Thomas Allen Hardin
Evelyn Harrand, née Lister
Michael J G Harris
Hazel M Hart
Mr Geoffrey P J Harvey
Mr & Mrs David Hastings
David E Hawes
Geoffrey Hawker
William Franklin Haynes
Mr K G Hazell
Peter E Heard
G W Hewett
R Holland
Iris Holmes (Mrs)
Malcolm Holmes
Mark Holmes
Michael & Barbara Hopkins
D M Howard
David George Huggins
Billy Hurt
Dan Hyde

Richard Jermy
Eric Johnson, Saugatuck, Michigan, USA
M P Jolly

Mrs B King
Mr Russ Klose
Mrs V P Knight
Nellie Knights, née Wilby
Jack & Dede Knox
S H Knudsen

C W Lakey
Barry James Lambert
Sylvia Kathleen Lancaster
Roy Larkins
Richard Robert Laxen
Ray & Jean Lemons
Derek Lilley
Richard Lindsay
Colin Robert Roy Ling
Rev Al Loades HCF

Mrs E M Marais
Fred Marlow
Luis Martinez Family, Laredo, Texas, USA
Trevor Mattocks
Philip Metcalfe
Mr & Mrs Trevor J Moore
Adrian Morris
A G Morris
D J Morris
Charles Mosgar USAAF

E H Nash
Mrs P G Norris

Mr D Osborne

Mr John Page
Mr P R Palmer
M J V Parker
Steven Parnell
Mr & Mrs David Patterson
Colin Peck
Mr A V B Peel
Peters-Lancaster Family
John Pigg
David Purple

Mr & Mrs Vince Re
Christopher Reeve
Russell A Reeve
Mr & Mrs James H Reeves
Eric N Rhodes
Mrs Daphne D Riches
Jack Rix
Mr D R Roberts
Keith Rogers
V G Rounce
I Rowarth
Mrs B Royal
Mrs J Rumble
Tony Runyeard
Yvonne Rutherford, née Osborne
Mr Godfrey Rutland

Peter B Sayer
Derek George Saywell
Mrs N K Scott

Brian E Self
Derek Ralph Self
David Seville
Mr J G & Mrs V A Shuck
Mrs S A Sirrell
Daphne Smith
Mrs M A Smith
Owen Smith-Jones
Mr E Steward
Bennie L Stewart
Bernard Stone
Sheila Street
Gary Surplice

Eric Gilbert Taylor
W J Taylor
David & Brenda Thompson
M A Thompson
J Thorpe
James Thorpe
Al Touchette, 467th Bomb Group, Rackheath - In Memory of Pvt Daniel Miney
Christopher Townsend
Mr I P Trumpess
T Tyrrell

Mr Jordan R Uttal

Alfonso L Valori
Mrs A L Vanham
B D P Vickers

Catherine R E Walker
Ralph Walker
W P S Watts
David White
John Wilds
Mrs S Wilkerson
Primrose Williams
M Williamson
L L G Willis
Ruth & Alf Wooltorton
Mrs D R Wynn

R Yarham

LIB-LAFFS

by ED HONMAN 491st

LIB-LAFFS

by ED HOHMAN 491st

448th BOMBARDMENT GROUP (H)

Presents

The 200th
Mission Celebration

A MESSAGE

THE achievements of the personnel of all units on this station which have permitted in a period of slightly more than one year the accomplishment of 200 Combat Missions against the enemy cannot be summed up in one short paragraph. Volumes will be required to record in the annals of the history of the Army Air Forces the difficulties encountered, the obstacles overcome, the losses incurred, the valor and heroism displayed, and the successes attained in the execution of each of these Missions. However, the accomplishment of 200 Combat Missions is in itself a milestone of our development, the passing of which is significant of the progress we have made toward our ultimate objective ; progress made possible as a result of the teamwork and co-ordination exhibited by both air and ground personnel. As such it presents not only an occasion worthy of commemoration and honorable celebration but also one which demands from each of us a renewal of his determination to redouble his efforts in the days to come in order that we may contribute in the best tradition of the service our full share toward final victory over the enemy.

CHARLES B. WESTOVER.

Colonel, Air Corps,
Commanding Officer

SATURDAY, 20th JANUARY. 1945
and
SUNDAY, 21st JANUARY, 1945

PROGRAM
y, 21st January, 1945

★ ★

... ...
how—The Terrie Sisters and   2-00 p.m.
e Brown, Fortune Teller

EA DANCE

... ...
thing Dance Orchestra   4-00 p.m.
... ...
atton Continentals   ...   4-00 p.m.
...
Flying Yanks   ...   4-00 p.m.

TAINMENT

... ...
SO Show   1-00 p.m. and 2-00 p.m.

...   4-00 p.m. and 6-30 p.m.
All-Canadian Stage Show

ACTIVITIES
(Permitting)

TIME : 2-00 P.M.

PLACE: Athletic Field adjacent to Site No. 4.
Bicycle Races will start at Site 4 Picket Post and finish at Aero Club.
1. EM Bicycle Race
2. Relay Team Bicycle Race   4. Mail Orderlies Race
3. Tug-of-War   5. " Milk Run " Race
                                    6. Pie-eating Contest
DINNER   7. Slow Bicycle Race (Majors only)
... ...
           All Mess Halls   5-00 to 7-30 p.m.
(All EM Women Guests and EM accompanied by ladies will
eat dinner in EM Mess No. 3.

★ ★

Trucks for departing guests will leave from the Gymnasium
at 8-30 p.m., Sunday, 21st January, 1945

OFFICERS CLUB, JANUARY 1944